The Official
GENERAL
HOSPITAL
Trivia Book

The Official
GENERAL
HOSPITAL
Trivia Book

Gerard J. Waggett

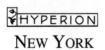

New York

Library of Congress Cataloging-in-Publication Data

Waggett, Gerard J.
    The official General Hospital trivia book / by Gerard
J. Waggett. — 1st ed.
        p. cm.
    ISBN 0-7868-8275-1
    1. General Hospital (Television program) I. Title
PN1992.77.G462W35 1997
791.45 ' 72—dc21   97–20747
                                                              CIP

DESIGNED BY HOLLY MCNEELY

FIRST EDITION

10 9 8 7 6 5 4 3 2 1

For Barbara, Jane, and Roseanne,
who introduced me to
GENERAL HOSPITAL

Contents

Acknowledgments

As always, my first debt of thanks goes to my editor, Gretchen Young. You have given me the chance to associate myself with one of my all-time favorite television shows. To my agents, Frank Coffey and Frank Weimann, thank you for looking out for my interests. To Gail Silverman and Sandra Dorsey at ABC, thank you for locating the pictures I needed.

My parents, Barbara and Fred Waggett, continue to be a source of support and encouragement. For their role in the overall picture, I would like to thank them, along with: Margaret, Jackie and Eddie Connolly, Mabel Waggett, Michael, his wife Christine, Kevin, Freddy and his wife Keri, and my nieces, Norma and Taylor.

A number of other people have contributed to this book in some way or another and deserve thanks: Scott Reedy, Angie Davito, and Irene Keene, for providing me with information; Don Casali, for listening to me talk about the book as much as he did; Eileen Maher and Jamie Walsh, for asking how the book was coming and meaning it; Bill Farrell, for being the first guy in high school to admit that he watched the soaps; and of course, Jane Hansen, Barbara Hansen, and Roseanne Montgomery for getting me hooked on *General Hospital* in the first place.

Introduction

I was about fifteen years old when I first started watching *General Hospital* in 1978, right before Tony Geary joined the show as Luke Spencer. I had stopped by my friend Jane Hansen's house on the way home from school just to say hi. As Jane pulled open the door, she shouted, "Bobbie's not pregnant!" From where I was standing, I could see her older brother Bobby spread out across the living floor watching TV. "Was there any doubt?" I asked and stepped inside. Of course, the Bobbie she was talking about was Jacklyn Zeman's Bobbie Spencer, whose whole pregnancy scam was unraveling in front of her. Shushed by Jane's mother, I sat down on the couch next to Jane's older sister Barbara, the one who had gotten Jane and her whole family into *General Hospital*. After a couple weeks of stopping by a couple of days a week and listening to Jane and Roseanne talk about Scotty and Laura, I started to care about whether Laura's parents would let the two of them get married. And I wanted to know who it was that Laura had killed.

By the following summer when I could watch the show every day, I was a full-blown addict. And in the fall of 1980, I developed the most perfectly timed case of food poisoning in my life. It kept me out of school for the entire week that Luke brought down the Frank Smith mob.

Collected here are a dozen of my own favorite scenes,

episodes, and story lines from *General Hospital* since I started watching back in 1978. I have listed them in chronological order.

The Lesley/Rick/Monica/Alan quadrangle (1979). Lesley delivering Monica's baby and hearing her call it Rick's son; the nursery ceiling collapsing on Alan, Rick, and Monica; Alan stalking Rick and Monica along the waterfront; Alan revealing publicly that the baby was his and not Rick's; the argument when Lesley stopped being nice. . . . This was one of those rare story lines in which every plot twist was a highlight.

Tracy withholds Edward's heart medication (1980). That scene of Tracy staring out the glass balcony doors, telling her father what a beautiful night it was while he collapsed onto the carpet remains the best Friday cliffhanger the show has ever come up with.

The first time Luke and Laura went on the run (1980). This was the story that started the crime/adventure trend on daytime, yet it also contained the most romantic scene in the show's history: Luke and Laura dancing around Wyndham's department store after hours. The show also pulled off one of its most shocking plot twists with Sally, the transvestite hit man.

Who killed Diana Taylor? (1981). As I note in this book, the Diana Taylor murder mystery had one of the most chilling scenes I have ever seen on daytime: Heather Webber writing the name Anne on the kitchen floor using Diana's own blood and lifeless arm. Robin Mattson's performance as Heather, especially the chemistry between her and Doug Sheehan as good guy private eye Joe Kelly, was one of the most fascinating in daytime history.

Scotty catches the bouquet (1981). A lot of curious people tuned in to Luke and Laura's wedding to see special guest Elizabeth Taylor. While she certainly had a presence, the real kick for me was that other gate-crasher. Scotty catching Laura's bouquet was the best-timed entrance any soap character has ever had returning to a show.

Luke and Laura's reunion (1983). Even when I recently watched the videotape, *Luke and Laura, Vol. 2: The Greatest Love of All,* that scene of Luke and the presumed-dead Laura running into each other's arms for the first time still gets to me.

Laura carries Lucky up the stairs (1994). There was one scene where the mob came after Laura and Lucky in General Hospital. Unable to walk, Lucky had to be carried by Laura up several flights of stairs while hit men stalked them. The episode worked on a number of levels. On the surface, it was an action story, but beneath that it was about the strength of a mother's love and commitment to protecting her child at any cost. Lucky was not a little boy; he was heavy. And Genie Francis's obvious difficulty in carrying him lifted the moment far above the typical chase scene.

BJ's heart transplant (1994). I cannot think of a plotline or moment on the show that has moved me closer to tears than the image of Tony Jones listening to his dead daughter's heart beating in her cousin Maxie's chest.

Lucy's striptease at the Nurses' Ball (1995). In one way or another, she'd taken off her clothes for money several times over the years, but never as entertainingly as she did during the second Nurses' Ball. This was Lynn Herring (*Lucy Coe*) at the top of her game: sexy, playful, and funny. I hit the rewind button several times.

Monica's breast cancer (1995). From start to finish, Monica's battle with breast cancer is painfully on target and the best work to date from a really talented actress, Leslie Charleson. One moment, though, clicked with me above all the rest. Disgusted with all the clothes that no longer fit, Monica tries to clear them away with a sweep of her arm, which pulls at her incision. Monica's reaction to this unexpected burst of pain interrupting her anger lifts the moment to a whole different level.

Robin's HIV diagnosis (1995). I literally felt as though I had been kicked in the gut when Alan stopped by Sonny's apartment to tell Robin that she'd tested HIV positive.

The return of the Cassadines (1997). When I first heard that Luke and Laura were returning to *General Hospital,* I was a little worried. These sort of returns rarely live up to expectation. But this was one of those rarities. And the return of the Cassadine family has been the can't-miss-a-day high point from their new history.

The Official
GENERAL
HOSPITAL
Trivia Book

The Early Days

*G*eneral Hospital was the network's first successful afternoon soap opera. In 1960, ABC had tried to launch an astronaut-themed serial titled *The Clear Horizon*, which featured future *General Hospital* leading lady Denise Alexander as the show's teen heroine. The show ran exactly seven months, was pulled from the afternoon lineup, and returned a year later for another four months. A few months after *Clear Horizon* debuted, ABC premiered *Road to Reality*, which dramatized group therapy sessions and lasted just under six months.

General Hospital was loosely based on ABC's primetime medical drama, *Ben Casey*, which had debuted in 1961 and was sitting comfortably in the top ten during the 1962–63 season. As such, it is probably no coincidence that *General Hospital*'s first leading man, John Beradino (*Dr. Steve Hardy*) bore a passing resemblance to Vince Edwards, who played Ben Casey.

In the planning stages, *General Hospital* was titled *Emergency Hospital*.

ABC Head of Daytime Armand Grant did not envision *General Hospital* as a soap opera during the planning stages.

He saw the show as self-contained, each episode having a beginning, middle, and end. In the original bible for the show, there were four main characters: a doctor, a nurse, an ambulance driver, and a police officer. Each afternoon would bring a new emergency. The bible was put together by Elizabeth Lewis, who had written for the prime-time series.

Armand Grant changed his mind about *Emergency Hospital* after learning that NBC was planning to launch the exact same sort of show on April 1, 1963—the same day *Emergency Hospital* was to have premiered. Rather than drop *Emergency Hospital*, Grant revamped the show into the soap format and retitled the project *General Hospital*. Ironically, *The Doctors* turned into a soap opera by the end of its first year on the air.

John Beradino wasn't too keen about signing a contract that would tie him up for five years, but his agent convinced him, by assuring him that the show would not run more than six months.

Emily McLaughlin, who played Nurse Jessie Brewer, was one of the first actresses to play a doctor on daytime. She was Dr. Eileen Seaton on the medical drama *Young Dr. Malone* from 1959 to 1960.

The show's director/producer Jim Young had also worked on *Young Dr. Malone* as a director.

Denise Alexander appeared in *GH*'s unaired pilot episode.

Three soap operas debuted on April 1, 1963: *General Hospital, The Doctors,* and the short-lived legal serial *Ben Jerrod*. Gerald Gordon, *GH*'s future Dr. Mark Dante, worked on all three soaps. Appearing on *Ben Jerrod* during its few months on the air were two other future *General Hospital* stars: Denise Alexander and Peter Hansen (*Lee Baldwin*).

Frank and Doris Hursley, who had been head writers for the highly successful CBS soap opera *Search for Tomorrow,* were hired to develop *General Hospital.* During *Search for Tomorrow*'s early days, much of the action took place at the hospital where the show's lead heroine Joanne Barron (Mary Stuart) worked. The Hursleys created *General Hospital* but remained at *Search for Tomorrow* while another husband and wife team, Theodore and Mathilde Ferro, wrote *GH* for the first six months. The Hursleys met with the Ferros once a week to discuss the story lines.

Before the first episode even aired, John Beradino took a cut in his salary so that more money could be put toward the sets.

The first episode of *General Hospital*, which ran half an hour, took twenty-two hours to tape.

Lucille Wall came onto the show two months into its run as tough nurse Lucille March. (The character was named after her.) Wall, who had played the lead role in the radio soap *Portia Faces Life*, was terrified of working on television.

General Hospital was a risky departure from soap operas of the time as defined by the powerhouse CBS line-up—*As the World Turns, Search for Tomorrow,* and *The Guiding Light*—which dealt with families. *General Hospital* shifted the focus from the kitchen table to the operating table. *General Hospital* debuted without a soap opera staple: the multigenerational family.

Unlike soaps at that time, which broke for commercials five times during a half hour period, *General Hospital* only broke for commercials three times, which allowed the writers to create longer scenes.

Unlike other soaps, the show was taped and not aired live. Although it was taped, actors were expected to get the scene down the first time. The camera never

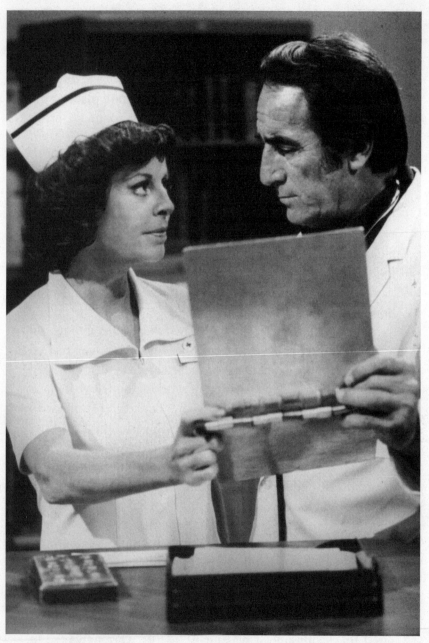

Many fans wanted to see Jessie Brewer (Emily McLaughlin) paired up
with the strong but caring Steve Hardy (John Beradino). 1975/ABC

If not for John Beradino's slip to the press, Audrey Hardy (Rachel Ames, left) would have been killed off. 1972/ABC

A former radio actress, Lucille Wall (*Lucille March*) was terrrified of working on television. (Also pictured, Rachel Ames, who played Lucille's sister, Audrey.) 1974/ABC

stopped rolling to give the actors a chance for a second take.

Getting things down on one take forced Beradino to think on his feet. In one scene, he pressed the button for the elevator, the doors of which were at that time operated by a crew member pulling on a rope. When only one door opened, Beradino ad-libbed, "Get maintenance to repair that elevator right away!"

One of the few times a scene was reshot was when Lucille March was speaking on the phone at the nurses' station. While she did, a small fire broke out behind her desk. After a minute or two of coughing but still trying to get through the scene, she broke character to ask the director, "Should I keep talking or put out the fire?" Crew members rushed in to extinguish the fire before it got out of control, and the scene continued.

After the show switched over to cordless microphones, every time a police cruiser drove by the studio, the microphones would pick up and broadcast the radio calls. Whatever the actor wearing the mike was saying would be drowned out. Since scenes were not retaped, the audience would hear the police call but not the actor's line.

Dr. Franz Bauer was hired to consult not only on the show's appearance and day-to-day details but on the scripts as well. The Hursleys prided themselves on the fact that they never resorted to the soap opera clichés of fictional diseases.

For the first few years on the air, *General Hospital*'s setting was never specified. The town was not named Port Charles, nor pinpointed in upstate New York, until the late 70s.

The show went to color in 1966.

The stress and long hours involved in putting *General Hospital* together day after day took its toll on the show's two stars, John Beradino and Emily McLaughlin, both of whom developed stomach ulcers as a result. McLaughlin's ulcers grew so severe that she required hospitalization.

Audrey March Hardy (played by Rachel Ames) was never intended to be a long-term role. The character was scheduled to die from lymphoma shortly after marrying Steve Hardy. When John Beradino let that piece of information slip to the press, the show's fans wrote in demanding that Audrey live. The story line was rewritten. Rachel Ames has now become the longest running actress in the show's history and one of the ten longest in the history of daytime television.

After Beradino spilled the beans about Audrey's impending death, the writers and producers were careful not to let him know too much about upcoming plot twists.

The 1970s

General Hospital received its highest pre–Gloria Monty ratings during the 1971–72 season when Audrey Hardy went on trial for murder.

John Beradino, as Steve Hardy, sang "Oh Promise Me" at Lucille March's wedding to Al Weeks. The song was a surprise not only to Lucille March, the character, but to Lucille Wall, the actress, as well, who cried real tears.

During the early '70s, *General Hospital* was so popular that ABC decided to launch a second medical soap, which the network intended to title *City Hospital*. Future *General Hospital* head writer Claire Labine and her writing partner Paul Avila Mayer played around with the show's premise and shifted the focus away from the hospital itself to a family-owned Irish pub across the street. The result was *Ryan's Hope*.

The Hursleys stepped down as head writers in the mid-'70s, passing on that responsibility to their daughter Bridget, who had been writing the show with them, and her husband, Jerome Dobson.

Among the teams replacing the Dobsons were the husband and wife team of Eileen and Robert Mason Pollock,

Steve Hardy (John Beradino) married Audrey March (Rachel Ames) for the second time in 1976. Also pictured here: Peter Hansen (*Lee Baldwin*), David Comfort (*Tommy Hardy*), and Emily McLaughlin (*Jessie Brewer*). 1976/ABC

who had been writing for *The Doctors* during its peak of popularity, and who would go on to become the head writers for the prime-time serial *Dynasty*.

In July 1976, *General Hospital* and its follow-up show *One Life to Live* switched time slots. During that switch, both shows were expanded from a half hour to forty-five minutes. They remain the only two soaps to ever run at the forty-five minute length.

By the mid-'70s, the public seemed to have lost interest in medical dramas. The once top-rated *Marcus Welby, M.D.* and *Medical Center* had disappeared from prime-time. On daytime, the two shows that had slipped the most in the ratings during this time were *General Hospital* and *The Doctors*.

In 1976, two characters came back from the dead: Rick Webber and Tom Baldwin. Rick had been presumed killed in a plane crash in Africa but had in fact been taken prisoner by revolutionaries who'd mistaken him for a CIA agent. Tom Baldwin, presumed killed south of the border, was actually sitting in a Mexican prison for a murder he did not commit.

Attempted suicide was an extremely popular plot device between 1976 and 1977. Jeff Webber shot himself in the head while losing his wife Monica to his own brother. Audrey Hardy overdosed on sleeping pills after losing her husband, Dr. Jim Hobart, who walked out on her. Mary Ellen Dante slashed her wrists to keep husband Mark Dante from leaving her for Terri Webber. And Heather Grant faked a suicide attempt to win Jeff's sympathy and affection.

In 1977, ABC head of programming Fred Silverman gave the show six months to bring the ratings up by at least two points or be canceled.

To boost ratings, the writers came up with a disaster story line: an intense hurricane that hit Port Charles and caused a blackout at the hospital. In one of the more interesting visuals, the doctors were forced to perform surgery in the parking garage, which was lit only by the headlights of the cars around them.

At one point, during the late '70s, episodes of *General Hospital* were being taped only a week before they aired.

Jacklyn Zeman's first day on *General Hospital* was days after her last day on *One Life to Live*. Fans of both shows saw Zeman (as *Lana McClain*) die from an overdose on *One Life*, then walk out of the elevator as Bobbie within the next week.

Head of ABC Daytime Jackie Smith figured out that bringing in new, young viewers was the best way to improve the ratings. *All My Children* and *The Young and the Restless*, which prominently featured young characters and targeted a young audience, had climbed into the top five soaps. Jackie looked for guidance from her own teen daughter, who preferred *The Doctors* to *General Hospital* because *The Doctors* focused on younger cast members. Smith then lured *The Doctors'* head writer, Doug Marland, to write for *General Hospital.*

Jackie Smith hired Gloria Monty, who had directed *The Secret Storm* in the '50s and *Bright Promise* in the '60s. After *Bright Promise*, Monty swore that she would never work on another soap opera. She had been working on ABC's Wide World mystery specials when Smith contacted her about producing *General Hospital.*

Monty and Marland were considered risky hires. Marland had only been writing for soaps for five years, far less as a head writer. *All My Children* and *One Life to Live* creator Agnes Nixon, who was acting at the time as a consultant for all the ABC soaps, advised Smith to give him the job after she'd seen the story outlines he had come up with. When Smith hired Monty, she had soap experience, but she had not worked on one in almost ten years and never as a producer.

Gloria Monty began producing *General Hospital* on New Year's Day, 1978.

Doug Marland once picked Tracy Quartermaine as his favorite among the characters he had created for the show. Around that same time, the show was expanded to a full hour.

Her very first day on the job, Gloria Monty reviewed four episodes that had already been taped and decided that they needed to be retaped—at a cost of $100,000.

The very first performer Monty hired was Anna Lee,

whom Monty, a film buff, remembered from Anna's extensive movie career.

After finding a number of tape-editing machines that were not being used, Monty dropped the "live tape" format, in which the show was taped in the exact order in which it was seen by the viewers. Instead scenes would be taped and then edited before broadcast, allowing the pauses that slowed the scenes down to be cut out and scenes to be broken down into smaller ones.

Following Monty's lead, the directors kept the actors physically moving during their scenes to maintain a high energy level and keep the scenes more visually stimulating.

Between 1978 and 1979, *General Hospital* jumped from number nine to number two in the ratings—the biggest leap any soap had ever made in one season.

ABC spent one million dollars building a new studio specifically to tape the show. The Gower Studio was the largest studio ever devoted to taping one soap opera.

Gloria Monty hired several actors with whom she had worked on the soap opera *Bright Promise*: Susan Brown (*Gail Adamson*), David Lewis (*Edward Quartermaine*), and Tony Geary (*Luke Spencer*). Monty had also worked with Geary in the TV thriller *Sorority Kill*.

Monty had originally discussed with Geary the idea of playing corrupt district attorney turned state senator Mitch Williams. When they realized that he wasn't really right for that part, the role of Luke Spencer was created for him. Luke was supposed to be a short-term role. He was to be killed off while trying to assassinate Mitch Williams, the role he had turned down. When Geary's Luke proved extremely popular with the fans, the story line was rewritten.

General Hospital's crime drama stories were attracting not only more young people but more male viewers as well.

Luke Spencer (Tony Geary), pictured here with his Aunt Ruby (Norma Connolly) and sister Bobbie (Jacklyn Zeman), was not originally created as a long-term role. 1980/ABC

Doug Marland wrote the Los Angeles–based *General Hospital* from his home in Connecticut. He would spend hours each day on the phone with Gloria Monty and would head out to California for meetings that sometimes lasted several weeks. He eventually left the show after Gloria Monty insisted that he move out to Los Angeles on a permanent basis. After that, he worked solely on East Coast shows: *Guiding Light*, *Loving*, and *As the World Turns*.

Amid talk that Genie Francis would be leaving *General Hospital* after Laura married Scotty, the character of Laura's adoptive sister Amy Vining (played by Shell Kepler) was introduced as a possible new young heroine for the show. Had Francis left, Monty had worked up an ice-skating story that would have taken Amy to the 1980 Winter Olympics in Lake Placid.

For their honeymoon, Scotty and Laura went to Hollywood. Since *General Hospital* is produced there, location footage of the honeymoon required the crew to take their cameras outside.

Marland and Monty had clashed over the Luke and Laura relationship. Marland wanted the newly wed Laura to enjoy her marriage to Scotty for a little while before trouble set in. Monty wanted to keep up the momentum with more conflict for Laura.

Pat Falken Smith, who replaced Doug Marland, came to *General Hospital* from *Days of Our Lives*, which had done quite well with a rape-triggered romance between two doctors. The name of the *Days* heroine who eventually married the man who raped her was Laura Spencer. Tony Geary had also played a rapist on *The Young and the Restless* in the early '70s before taking on the role of Luke Spencer, who raped Laura Baldwin.

Pat Falken Smith, who had replaced Marland as head writer on *General Hospital*, also replaced him as head writer on *Guiding Light*.

Two real-life figures played themselves on a recurring basis on the show: fitness expert Richard Simmons, who ran workout classes mornings at the Campus Disco; and psychologist Irene Kassorla, who ran marriage counseling sessions that Lesley Webber attended. Both Simmons and Kassorla landed books on *The New York Times* best-seller list after appearing on the show. In the '90s, Kassorla would return to the show as herself to counsel Dominique Taub (Shell Danielson).

General Hospital became the number one–rated soap

opera on daytime in 1979, a position it would hold for nine years.

Film buff Monty lifted the image of Luke and Laura sleeping in the same room with a blanket hanging between them from the Frank Capra comedy *It Happened One Night*.

After the October 1980 scene in which Luke and Laura took down the blanket between them and finally made love, fans called in complaining that the scene was neither long nor explicit enough.

At one point, Monty herself had taken ill and needed to be hospitalized. A closed-circuit TV monitor was set up in her hospital room so that she could watch the show being filmed. Her doctor noticed that her blood pressure rose whenever she was watching the monitor and ordered it to be removed from her room.

The 1980s

*O*n 1981, with the show comfortably on top of the Nielsens, Monty wanted to do something that had never been done before on daytime—science fiction. Head writer Pat Falken Smith warned Jackie Smith that the Ice Princess story line would ruin the show. Despite Falken Smith's predictions, the show's ratings skyrocketed during the Ice Princess story line.

After *General Hospital* head writer Doug Marland took over as head writer at *Guiding Light*, he hired Jane Elliot to play a character with multiple personalities. *Guiding Light* fired her before the story line was finished and Marland left the show when his contract ended.

Gloria Monty enjoyed working on science fiction. One of the movies for ABC's Wide World of Entertainment series she had been most proud of was the science fiction story "Jack 243."

Scenes from Prince Charles's wedding to Diana were shown on *General Hospital*. On board the yacht, the Cassadines watched a videotape of the wedding, since their plans to conquer the world kept them from attending.

After the Ice Princess story line proved so successful,

The Ice Princess adventure redefined soap operas in the 1980s.
Pictured here: Tony Geary and Genie Francis (*Luke* and *Laura*.)
1981/ABC

other soap operas came up with their own science fiction
story lines. *One Life to Live* reintroduced an old villain as a
mad scientist, who implanted mind control devices inside
victims' brains. *Days of Our Lives* created its own
Cassadine-like family, the DiMeras, one of whom was
played by Thaao Penghliss, who had played Victor
Cassadine. One of the show's story lines had Stefano
(Joseph Mascolo) hunting for magic prisms that could grant

him immortality. On *The Doctors*, one of the show's final story lines before cancellation dealt with an elixir for eternal youth.

General Hospital was the cover story of the September 28, 1981, issue of *Newsweek*. The cover photo showed Genie Francis and Tony Geary in an island scene from the Ice Princess story line. The week of Luke and Laura's wedding, *People* magazine put Genie Francis, Tony Geary, and Elizabeth Taylor on the cover; it was the second biggest-selling issue of the magazine that year. (The best-selling issue featured the year's other popular bride, Princess Diana.) Demi Moore had been on *General Hospital* for only a few weeks before she and Tony Geary landed on the cover of *US* magazine.

Luke and Laura married on November 16 and 17, 1981. Some 30 million fans tuned in, setting a new and as yet unbroken record for daytime soap viewing.

Although thrilled with the show's success, Gloria Monty was a little melancholy over it following the wedding. "I have nowhere to go but down," she was quoted as saying.

Genie Francis announced that she would be leaving the show shortly after the wedding. As part of the story line surrounding Laura's departure, look-alike Janine Turner was cast as Laura Templeton. The villainous David Gray (Paul Rossilli) attacked a number of young blond women named Laura. The fact that David Gray shared the same last name as Laura's biological father, Gordon Gray, had several long-time fans wondering if there was some connection between David and Laura, but the naming was merely coincidental.

After playing around with science fiction in the Ice Princess story line, the Sword of Malkuth saga combined science fiction with the supernatural. Among the supernatural touches to the story line were David's skills at hypnosis, the Cassadine curse that was placed on Luke and Laura, and Luke's sudden development of psychic abilities. Luke ultimately killed David Gray by pointing the Sword of Malkuth at him and willing him out a window. Added to that, the story line also involved holography.

Tristan Rogers once picked the Sword of Malkuth story as his least favorite to play.

After newcomer Steve Bond (*Jimmy Lee Holt*) was wardrobed in nothing but a pair of briefs for several of his scenes early on, the censors stepped in and demanded that in any future underwear scenes, he wear boxer shorts.

The show's twentieth anniversary fell on Good Friday in 1983.

Laura's return to Port Charles was perfectly scheduled for Friday, November 11, 1983. Since the day was Veterans Day, many fans of the show were at home and planned to watch. *TV Guide,* which very rarely mentioned any blurb for soaps under its daily listings, mentioned that Genie Francis would be returning to the show that day. As it turned out, a newsbreak a few days before had thrown ABC's afternoon schedule off-kilter. Laura's return was not seen until the following Monday.

During Genie Francis's return, *General Hospital* experimented with airing teasers at the end of the episode—a convention that did not become commonplace on the show until 1997.

The 1983 downing of a Korean Air Lines 747 by Soviet missiles inspired a story in which a television clown, whose sister died in a similar crash caused by the DVX, sought vengeance on former DVX agent Grant Andrews. What made the story line all the more interesting for daytime was that it was self-contained. The character was introduced in the first segment and had been arrested by the last—very similar to prime-time crime dramas.

When Tony Geary chose to leave the show in early 1984, the show devoted an entire episode to his character saying good-bye. As Luke met each of his friends and family one-on-one, the characters reminisced about old times. Luke also visited a couple of his old stomping grounds, including the Campus Disco he used to run, which was now boarded up. Flashback clips were intercut with scenes of Luke walking around Port Charles.

Genie Francis and Tony Geary returned for a few weeks during the fall of 1984. Geary was used quite heavily during that time, helping Robert Scorpio chase down a stolen Aztec treasure on location in Mexico. Francis had taped only a handful of episodes, which were placed sporadically throughout the story line. Laura had stayed back on the hacienda while Luke and Robert had their adventure. During Luke and Laura's reunion, Laura told Luke that she was pregnant.

In 1985, the geography of Port Charles was extended to include an Asian quarter.

After Aaron Spelling hired Emma Samms to take over the role of Fallon on *Dynasty*, she balanced her taping schedule for the two shows. To accommodate Samms and lessen her workload during her final few months, Holly was kidnapped and held prisoner for weeks on end.

When Anna Devane was first introduced, the character wore her hair over the side of her face to cover a disfiguring scar. While the scar added a nice touch to the character when she was being played as a villainess, the producers also recognized in Finola Hughes great potential as a leading lady. Rather than waste any time with an extended plastic surgery story line, the scar was simply peeled off on screen. Anna, it was revealed, had been wearing the fake scar as penance for the sins she had committed in the past.

Anna was originally going to be paired romantically with the unorthodox Dr. Buzz Stryker (Don Galloway). Although the two were likeable enough as friends, they didn't share the level of chemistry that a character of Anna's dimension merited. The Anna/Buzz relationship was therefore shelved and the character of mobster Duke Lavery was created.

When Gloria Monty left as producer in 1986, she was replaced by H. Wesley Kenney, who had been producing the number-two-rated soap, *The Young and the Restless.* Ironically, it was during this period that *The Young and the Restless* supplanted *General Hospital* as the most popular soap opera on daytime.

By the time that the Mount Rushmore conclusion to the 1987 spy wars story was being taped, the show was working against a tight deadline. A directors' strike had been announced to begin in three days. Within that time, the cast and crew managed to tape seventy-nine scenes, many of them complicated action sequences, including one on a speeding train.

In 1987, Tom and Simone Hardy became daytime's first interracial married couple. While other shows such as *Days of Our Lives* and *All My Children* had featured interracial couples, none of them had made it to the altar.

The censors stepped in again during the story line in which Grant Putnam planned to kidnap Robin Scorpio and lock her in a cage in his basement. According to rules concerning minors, it was not allowed for TV to show children in cages of any sort, so the plotline had to be reworked. It was Anna and not Robin who wound up locked up in Grant's basement.

Emma Samms (*Holly Scorpio*), pictured here with Tristan Rogers (*Robert Scorpio*), balanced jobs on *General Hospital* and *Dynasty* during the summer of 1985. 1983/ABC

Nancy Reagan contacted the show about borrowing a dress that Bobbie had worn during one of her weddings. Because the dress had been custom-made for Jacklyn Zeman to wear, it could not be properly altered for the First Lady.

One of the most difficult characters to cast in the '80s was Dawn Winthrop, a daughter that Monica had given up for adoption years ago. In less than two years, the show had hired four different actresses to play the part. Eventually, Dawn was killed off.

One of the odder recasting decisions was that of Duke Lavery. Ian Buchanan, who had left the show in the late '80s as Duke was presumed killed in a fire, came back for a few episodes to expedite a plastic surgery story line that would introduce a new actor as Duke. Gregory Beecroft, who had just been killed off on *As the World Turns,* was seen playing Duke as the bandages came off his face. The show had gone to so much trouble recasting the role that many fans were more than a little shocked when he was shot and killed a few months later. Gregory Beecroft holds the distinction of being one of the few soap actors to be killed on-screen twice in one year playing major characters.

In 1990, the geography of Port Charles was expanded yet again to include a Hispanic section of town.

During the '80s, other shows had by and large followed *General Hospital*'s lead, introducing science fiction. *General Hospital*'s lead-in *One Life to Live* had gone so far as to send one character a hundred years into the past to the Old West and had constructed an underground city. As if not to be outdone by imitators, in 1990, *General Hospital* launched its most unusual story line to date. An alien from outer space landed in Anna Devane's backyard and befriended her daughter Robin.

Among the special effects required by the Casey the Alien story line, fiber optics were attached to Bradley Lockerman's fingernails to give the effect that Casey's fingers glowed.

The 1990s

*G*loria Monty returned as executive producer in late 1990. Although she was the one who had begun the science fiction era on daytime, this time around she moved the show away from the science fiction/adventure format and tried to redefine the show as being about class struggle. To do that, she introduced a new core family, the working-class Eckerts, to counterbalance the old money Quartermaines.

To make room for new characters, roughly a dozen lead and supporting characters were written off the show within Monty's first few weeks on the job.

As if to symbolize the major changes going on in the early '90s, a major earthquake hit Port Charles. The earthquake also justified rebuilding a number of the sets. Three years later, Los Angeles was hit with a major earthquake, which flooded the *General Hospital* studio.

Emily McLaughlin died in 1991 from cancer. During her last years with the show, her appearances had grown fewer and further between.

Because Finola Hughes's contract expired before the end of her story line and couldn't be extended due to a scheduling conflict, the role of Anna had to be recast in her

In a daring move, head writer Claire Labine introduced AIDS into the teen love story of Stone and Robin (Michael Sutton and Kimberly McCullough). 1995/Craig Sjodin/ABC

final weeks. Camilla Moore, who had once played a secret agent on *Days of Our Lives,* took over the role.

Despite the fact that Gloria Monty had saved the show from cancellation in the late '70s and turned it into the number-one-rated soap, this time around, her changes did not help *General Hospital* reclaim the top spot.

Monty was replaced by Wendy Riche, who had never worked on a soap opera before. Her experience had come totally from developing series and movies for prime-time.

Lynn Herring's pregnancies have been worked into her

story lines in the most unusual ways. When she was pregnant with her first child, Lucy was allowed to get pregnant,
but since the writers didn't want to saddle her with a child,
Herring had to act out a miscarriage not long before she was
due to give birth in real life. Herring's second pregnancy
served as the catalyst for one of Lucy's best story lines: acting as a surrogate mother for Scotty and the dying
Dominique's baby.

The writers specifically introduced Jagger Cates
(Antonio Sabato Jr.) as a cigarette smoker and then had him
quit to send out the message to the young people tuning in
that cigarette smoking did not make a person cool.

General Hospital nearly lost one of its most popular vil-
lains when Jon Lindstrom was contacted to play the role of
Damian Grimaldi on *As the World Turns*. Rather than risk
recasting the role during a pivotal time in the story line, the
producers offered Lindstrom a contract. Since Ryan was
proving too villainous to simply let roam free, the writers created the character of Ryan's twin brother Kevin Collins, who
has emerged as one of the show's most popular characters.

In 1993, *Ryan's Hope* creator Claire Labine took over as
head writer and quickly turned *General Hospital* into the
most widely praised soap on TV. Like Doug Marland in the
1970s, Brooklyn resident Labine wrote the Los
Angeles–produced show from her East Coast home.

During Ned and Lois's wedding, the outside scenes of
which were filmed on location in Brooklyn, head writer
Claire Labine made a guest appearance as Lois's neighbor.
She was taped in front of her own brownstone home where
Ned and Lois's limousine had gotten stuck in traffic.

To celebrate the Day of Compassion (June 21), daytime
television has incorporated AIDS themes into its shows.
General Hospital was one of the first soaps to participate,

ABOVE The Annual Nurses' Ball combines music, comedy, poignance, education, and glamour. Pictured here: Kimberly McCullough (*Robin Scorpio*). 1996/Cathy Blaivas/ABC
NEXT PAGE, TOP Lynn Herring (*Lucy Coe*) and Mary Beth Evans (*Katherine Bell*). 1996/Cathy Blaivas/ABC
NEXT PAGE, BELOW Rosalind Cash (*Mary Mae Ward*), Joseph Phillips (*Justus Ward*), Jonathan Jackson (*Lucky Spencer*), and Tony Geary (*Luke Spencer*). 1995 Cathy Blaivas/ABC

running a hospital scene between Bobbie Jones and a woman living with the HIV virus. The following year, the show took the Day of Compassion several steps further and introduced the Nurses' Ball, an AIDS fundraiser that ran for the entire week of June 21. Since that time, the Nurses' Ball has become an annual event.

Introduced during the first Nurses' Ball was the character

John Hanley, who would recur on the show a number of times until his death. The AIDS-stricken John Hanley was played by Lee Mathis, who himself had AIDS. Before coming onto *GH*, Mathis had taken out an ad in the entertainment papers asking for work so that he could meet the minimum number of hours of employment the acting union required to continue his medical insurance. *General Hospital* was one of the places that responded to his request.

Stone's battle with AIDS and Robin's HIV diagnosis were heralded by *TV Guide* soap critic Michael Logan as the most important teen love story of all time. Stone Cates became one of the first existing characters on a soap to be diagnosed with AIDS. While other soaps had done AIDS stories, most of the characters who died from the disease had been brought on specifically for that story line.

ABC's *Afternoon Special* filmed an entire documentary about Robin and Stone's story. Titled "Positive: A Journey Into AIDS," the special followed Michael Sutton and Kimberly McCullough as they prepared for their ground-breaking story line.

The show scheduled Stone's memorial service to fall on December 1, recognized as World AIDS Day.

The producers added more than a touch of realism to Monica's battle with breast cancer by casting a number of cancer survivors as cancer patients in Monica's support group. Riley Steiner, a cervical cancer survivor, played Emily's late mother Paige Bowen. To make Monica's stay at the Wellness Center as true to life as possible, Wendy Riche, Claire Labine, and Charleson visited a number of Wellness Centers around the country.

The writers considered having Audrey Hardy develop Alzheimer's disease, but changed their minds because the

Monica's (Leslie Charleson) battle with breast cancer both drew Monica and Alan (Stuart Damon) closer together and pushed them further apart. 1995/Craig Sjodin/ABC

dual blow of Monica's breast cancer and Stone's death from AIDS had left the viewers a little too depressed.

On the show's thirtieth anniversary, a new opening segment was introduced that included the faces of all the contract players on the show as well as some scenes from past episodes. The ambulance siren was replaced with the instrumental jazz number "Faces of the Heart" by Dave Koz.

Returning briefly for the thirtieth anniversary was Jana Taylor, who had played Angie, the show's first teen heroine, from 1963–65. Angie was also Steve Hardy's first patient. When Angie ran into Steve at the hospital on April 1, 1993, they reminisced about their first meeting, highlighted by clips from that first episode where Angie's burn-scarred face was wrapped in bandages.

The character of Mike Corbin, played by Ron Hale, was only supposed to last a few months. Mike was scripted to be killed, taking a bullet meant for his estranged son, Sonny Corinthos. A few weeks before the shooting was to be taped, Wendy Riche called Hale into her office and asked him if he would be willing to stay on. Mike still took a bullet for Sonny but survived his act of heroism.

Former head writers Claire and Matthew Labine had an affinity for animal stories. They were the ones who created the star-crossed romance between family dogs Annabelle Quartermaine and Foster Spencer that included the soap staple of the surprise pregnancy. They also gave Lucy a pet duck. Recently the Labines took over head writing duties at *OLTL*; one of their first moves was to give lead villian and loner Todd Manning (Roger Howarth) a parrot to talk to.

Luke and Laura celebrated their fifteenth anniversary on November 15, 1996, because the sixteenth and seventeenth fell on a Saturday and Sunday that year. The show was dedicated to the two of them and included a number of clips from their story lines over the years.

On Saturday night, December 14, 1996, *General Hospital* aired its very first prime-time episode—which was subtitled "Twist of Fate." The show revolved around the funeral for the presumed dead Laura Webber and ended with Stefan Cassadine accidentally shooting Katherine Bell.

A special issue of *TV Guide* in 1996 picked Luke and Laura's wedding as one of the 101 most memorable moments in television history. The fortieth anniversary issue of the magazine a few years before had named the show the top daytime soap of all time.

John Beradino, the last remaining original cast member

on the show, died in 1996. In the previous months, the show had lost Rosalind Cash (*Mary Mae Ward*) to cancer and Lee Mathis, who recurred as John Hanley, to AIDS.

Although Beradino died in the spring, Steve Hardy did not die until the summer. The show remembered Beradino and Steve with a memorial service filled with clips dating back to the show's early days. The episode ended with a montage of Beradino's scenes while Jimmy Durante's version of "Make Someone Happy" played in the background. Out of respect to Beradino's long-term contributions to the show, his face has been left in the opening credits, at least for a while.

In 1996, *General Hospital* taped its 8,500th episode.

In 1997, *General Hospital* began opening with a recap of the previous day in order to bring the viewer who may have missed an episode up to speed on what was going to happen in that day's episode. The show also began ending its shows with teasers for the following day.

General Hospital participated in ABC's March Against Drugs campaign by stepping up several of its drug-related story lines during March 1997. Emily began experimenting with drugs to deal with the stress of living in the Quartermaine household; Brenda Barrett admitted that she had become dependent upon the pills she had been taking for her back pain. The audience also saw that her doctor, Alan Quartermaine, Brenda's doctor and Emily's adoptive father, was popping pills to handle the stress around him. Amber Tamblyn, who played Emily, taped a public service announcement encouraging parents to talk to their kids about drugs.

General Hospital can now be seen in countries all around the world, including New Zealand, Germany, Italy, Latin America, Spain, the Middle East, and North Africa.

Backstage Stories

*W*ith the tension around the set so high so often, John Beradino could not suffer actors showing up for work late and ill-prepared for their scenes. Rather than take out his frustration and anger on his cast mates, Beradino would often take it out on the sets. Twice, he punched his fist right through the door to Steve Hardy's office. While the wood used for the door was plywood, the third time that the show had to replace the door, an oak door was bought. But nobody remembered to point this out to Beradino. The next time he got riled up and punched the door to Steve's office, he broke his own hand.

During one scene, Phil Brewer (Roy Thinnes) examined a patient and then headed out of the room. By the time Roy Thinnes had left, the extra let out a scream. As it turned out, Thinnes's ankle had become entangled in the extra's microphone wire, which strangled the man as Phil left the room. But the tape did not stop running. (The extra was fine.)

Both Stuart Damon and Leslie Charleson (*Alan* and *Monica Quartermaine*) have had trouble walking away from tables during different scenes. As Alan stood up to leave the cafeteria, his trench coat stuck to his chair, and he ended up carrying the chair out with him. Monica was trying to leave a restaurant when her purse got hooked to a chair and dragged it several feet. Charleson made light of the flub by apologizing to the chair. Both scenes needed to be retaped.

When Richard Simmons joined the cast as himself to teach exercise classes on camera, he also taught them behind the scenes as well. Among the cast members who showed up for his 7:30 A.M. exercise class were Stuart Damon, Jacklyn Zeman, and Kin Shriner. Simmons helped one cast member, Vanessa Brown (*Mrs. DeFreest*), lose thirty-five pounds.

Liz Keifer, who was introduced as Sister Camellia in 1986, found that people tended to treat her differently while she walked around backstage in her character's habit. Laughter stopped when she entered a room and subjects of conversation tended to change. Actors, especially the extras, she noticed, would sit up straighter when she passed by them.

While *General Hospital* was taping on location at Mt. Rushmore, a tourist recognized Sharon Wyatt, who played former movie star Tiffany Hill. Not realizing that the camera was rolling, the woman walked right into the scene, saying, "Look, it's Tiffany." The quick-thinking Wyatt saved the crew the trouble of a reshoot by incorporating the woman into the scene. "You must recognize me from my movies," Wyatt ad-libbed and smoothly escorted the woman out of the way.

David Groh let his temper get the best of him in a scene in which his character, D.L. Brock, rescued Bobbie Spencer (Jacklyn Zeman) from a pair of thugs along the docks. Caught up in the passion of the scene, Groh deviated from the script and yelled out an obscenity as the actors who played the thugs ran away from him. Rather than reshoot the scene, the producer chose to drown out Groh's expletive with a well-timed foghorn blast.

Brian Patrick Clarke and Sherilyn Wolter (*Grant Andrews* and *Celia Quartermaine*) were the classic pair of actors whom the audience loved to see together but who had more than a little trouble dealing with each other. Wolter had gone so far as to tell one soap publication that she wanted to punch Clarke's lights out. One time, she almost did. After months of playing the romance between Celia and Russian spy Grant Andrews, Wolter got to play some anger. Grant told Celia that he had never loved her and that he should have killed her as he had originally been ordered to do, and Celia responded by slapping him across the face. Whether it was months of built-up anger coming out or not, Wolter forgot to "pull her punch." The slap she gave Clarke left his ears ringing. The two, it should be noted, have gotten over that initial animosity and become friends.

John Reilly (*Sean Donely*) learned the hard way to watch out for his feet over the years. During the Mr. Big mob war story, one of the extras dropped a prop gun on Reilly's foot, breaking his big toe. Years later, while Sean was marrying Tiffany, the script called for Tiffany to stomp on Sean's foot. Sharon Wyatt did so with enough force to draw blood. She drove the heel of her shoe right through the top of Reilly's and into his foot.

Like most location shoots, the one at Big Bear had its share of accidents, minor and semi-major. On the boat to the island where Jason, Karen, and Jagger would be marooned, Cari Shayne was hit in the head with the camera more than a couple of times. Leif Riddell, who played escaped convict

Cal Atkins, broke his hand while rehearsing a fall off the cliff. Adding insult to injury, one of the stunt-men on the shoot fell from much higher up and walked away with only a scratch. To make Riddell feel better, executive producer Wendy Riche herself prepared him a peanut butter and jelly sandwich.

John J. York (*Mac Scorpio*) was called upon to help the producers audition the nine finalists for the role of Dominique Taub, which would eventually go to Tawney Feré Ellis. When he got there, he realized that the scene they were doing involved him getting slapped across the face— by each and every one of the nine actresses.

Shell Kepler (Amy Vining) provided her own dress for the 1996 Nurses' Ball. She dyed the wedding dress from her first marriage blue and wore it on the show.

The first day that Tyler Christopher (*Nikolas Cassadine*) was shooting, he got stuck in the elevator on the nurses' station set. He didn't realize that there was a secret door in the back through which the actors could exit once the elevator doors closed. So he waited there for a little while before someone came over to let him know that he didn't have to stay in there all day.

Amber Tamblyn (*Emily Quartermaine*) suffers from arachnophobia. When a scene called for Emily to pick up her pet tarantula, Tamblyn went to the writers and asked them if they would change the scene. She also suggested that the spider be killed off and Emily be given a rat, the sort of pet Tamblyn herself had at home.

During a trip to the wardrobe department, John Ingle (*Edward Quartermaine*) noticed that a pair of pajamas had been bought for him to wear on-screen, prompting him to ask whether Edward would be getting a bedroom scene in the near future. When the wardrobe person replied that he suspected Edward might be getting sick, Ingle felt a little panicky. "Am I going to die?" he asked. The wardrober assured him that Edward would not be dying soon by showing him all the new shirts that had been bought for the character.

Crossovers

*I*n 1968, John Beradino became one of the first actors to cross over from one soap opera to another. To give the fledgling *One Life to Live* a boost, Steve Hardy traveled to Llanview, Pennsylvania, to consult on a blood disorder afflicting *One Life to Live* heroine Meredith Lord (played at the time by Trish Van Devere).

In 1992, *One Life to Live*'s premiere con artist Marco Dane (Gerald Anthony), who had left Llanview years before, turned up in Port Charles. While posing as Ned Ashton, he introduced himself to Ned's mother, Tracy Quartermaine (Jane Elliot). Tracy hired him to investigate her daughter-in-law, Jenny Eckert Ashton (Cheryl Richardson). Marco also managed Jagger Cates's (Antonio Sabato Jr.) boxing career and dug up dirt on Tiffany Hill (Sharon Wyatt) for Bobbie Jones (Jacklyn Zeman) to use against her in a custody battle. Marco's extended stay in Port Charles earned Anthony a Best Supporting Actor Emmy.

One Life to Live lawyer Jonathan Russell (John Martin) traveled from Llanview to Port Charles to represent serial killer Ryan Chamberlain (Jon Lindstrom). He also gave legal advice to Lucy Coe (Lynn Herring).

Marco Dane had obviously infected Tracy Quartermaine with the crossover fever. After being disowned by her family in 1996, she headed off for Soho to take over the position of lead diva that was being vacated by Morgan Fairchild on ABC's *The City*. Shortly before Tracy left Port Charles, Sydney Chase (Morgan Fairchild) was seen on *General Hospital* during an intentionally brief phone conversation with Tracy.

One of *General Hospital*'s archcriminals, Cesar Faison (Anders Hove) turned up in Corinth, the setting for *Loving,* and kidnapped the show's comic heroine/vixen Ava Rescott (Lisa Peluso), who had accidentally stolen a priceless stamp from him. He then chased her and Jeremy Hunter (Jean LeClerc), himself a transplant from *All My Children*, all the way down to Universal Studios.

Inside Jokes

*D*uring one of Shell Kepler's first days as Amy Vining, she worked with Stuart Damon. While Stuart was giving Amy a tour of the Quartermaine mansion, she remarked, "I feel like Cinderella." The line, a subtle reference to Damon's role as Prince Charming in the 1965 TV broadcast of "Cinderella," cracked Kepler up.

There have been other funny television references. Once, on the NBC sitcom *Suddenly Susan,* Susan (Brooke Shields) was watching *General Hospital* and made a catty remark about Luke's hair. Soon after, *General Hospital* offered up a fun rebuttal.

Laura (to Luke, who is sitting in front of the TV set): *What are you watching?*

Luke: *I'm not sure. When did Brooke Shields become a comedienne? Did I sleep through that particular glitch in American history?*

Laura: *Her hair seems a little strange, don't you think?*

Luke: *Who am I to criticize other people's hair?*

Ned Ashton (Wally Kurth) ran into his pregnant ex-wife

Jenny (Cheryl Richardson) in the emergency room at General Hospital. When he asked where her husband, Paul Hornsby, was, she replied, "Savannah." In reality, Paul Satterfield, who played Paul, was working on the prime-time serial *Savannah*.

In a similar fashion, Sonny Corinthos asked new police detective Taggert, "Where's Garcia?" referring to Detective Alex Garcia, the role played by George Alvarez. Taggert replied, "He was transferred to Los Angeles." Alvarez had recently landed a role on the Los Angeles–based soap *The Bold and the Beautiful*.

When June Lockhart (*Maria*) was putting in a guest appearance during Felicia's first wedding to Frisco, the director thought it would make a nice touch to come back from commercial and have Lockhart dancing with her former *Lost in Space* co-star Mark Goddard, who played Derek Barrington on the show. A scene preceding their dance where they did a double take upon seeing each other for the first time was left on the cutting room floor.

While Tom Hardy was out of town, his girlfriend Felicia invited his mother over for dinner one Monday evening. "We can check out that cute doctor on *Melrose Place*," Felicia suggested. Felicia may have meant Michael Mancini, played by Thomas Calabro, but most fans assumed that she was talking about Peter Burns, played by Kristina Wagner's real-life husband Jack Wagner.

Getting Out of Town for a While

*L*ocation shoots have taken the show's film crew right outside their own door for Laura and Scotty's honeymoon in Hollywood, across the country for Lois and Ned's Brooklyn wedding, and across the Atlantic Ocean to Scotland for Duke and Anna's honeymoon. This quiz takes a look at some of the show's more notable location shoots. (Answers on page 194.)

1. A location shoot at Mt. Rushmore climaxed a spy story that found singer Dusty Walker hypnotized into assassinating secret agents and planting a bomb on a train that would be passing by an early warning system for nuclear weapons. What song was used as the trigger to put Dusty into his hypnotic trances?
  (a) "Live and Let Die" (b) "Sneak Attack"
  (c) "40 Million Stars" (d) "Don't Worry, Be Happy"

2. To celebrate what occasion did Ned and Lois ride the roller coaster at Coney Island?
  (a) the release of his first CD
  (b) his sold-out concert (c) their wedding
  (d) their first night of lovemaking

When Ned Ashton (Wally Kurth) offered to take Lois Cerullo (Rena Sofer) to any island she wanted, she picked Coney Island.
1994/Donna Svennevik

3. What were Frisco and Felicia searching for in the jungles of Mexico?

        (a) Aztec treasure   (b) their kidnapped baby

        (c) Felicia's long-lost father

        (d) a bag of stolen diamonds

4. Which of the following couples did not go to Puerto Rico during the 1995 location shoot?

        (a) Ned and Lois   (b) Sonny and Brenda

        (c) Damian and Katherine   (d) Miguel and Lily

Celebrity Guests

*E*lizabeth Taylor, a fan of *General Hospital* since her days living in Washington, D.C., as Senator John Warner's wife, had contacted the producers about doing a guest spot on the show. The writers quickly set about creating the character of Helena Cassadine, the widow of the mad scientist whom Luke Spencer (Tony Geary) had killed during the Ice Princess adventure. So quickly did the writers whip up a story line for Helena that they initially left out the one scene that the show's fans wanted to see: the confrontation between Helena and Luke. By the time Tony Geary brought the oversight to their attention, the problem had been corrected. Because of scheduling demands, Taylor was not able to tape scenes at the actual wedding. Instead, her scenes were taped afterwards and edited in.

Shortly after Elizabeth Taylor made her historic appearance, TV legend Milton Berle turned up as agent Mickey Miller, an acquaintance of Tiffany Hill. Mickey met Laura and convinced her to become a model. When Laura later turned up missing, Berle came back for Mickey to be questioned about the disappearance.

Soap fan Sammy Davis Jr. earned a 1980 Daytime

Emmy nomination as Best Cameo Appearance for his week-long stint as con man Chip Warren on *One Life to Live*. In the early '70s, he had also performed on the now-defunct soap *Love of Life*. He paid a week-long visit to *General Hospital* in 1982, playing Eddie Phillips, Bryan's (Todd Davis) long-lost father. Eddie, who was terminally ill, made peace with his son before dying.

During *General Hospital*'s early days, New York Yankees catcher Yogi Berra, who knew John Beradino from Beradino's days playing professional baseball, came on the show for a guest cameo as a brain surgeon. Berra didn't have any lines. He merely roamed the hallway in surgical scrubs while other characters made reference to him as the new brain surgeon, Dr. Berra.

In 1992, the year that the Buffalo Bills made it to the Superbowl, quarterback Jim Kelly, a fan of the show, made the trip from Buffalo to "nearby" Port Charles.

Housewives-turned-stand-up comics Caryl Kristensen and Marilyn Kentz have welcomed a number of actors from *General Hospital* onto their morning talk show *Caryl & Marilyn: Real Friends*. On the 1996 New Year's Eve episode, the show returned the favor, casting the pair as patrons at Luke's blues club. Kristensen had a little trouble with her lines once she spotted Stuart Damon, whom she'd had a crush on from his role as "Cinderella's" Prince Charming.

The singer/actress Sheila Macrae was best known as the wife of legendary singer Gordon Macrae, who'd starred in such musicals as *Oklahoma*. Fans of *The Honeymooners* remembered her as the actress who took over the role of Alice Kramden, wife to Jackie Gleason's Ralph Kramden, in a late '60s revival of the series. In 1991, she put in several guest appearances on *General Hospital* as Madelyn Richmond, wife to the town's mayor.

During Elizabeth Taylor's historic visit to daytime, the writers nearly forgot to include a meeting between Luke (Tony Geary) and Helena Cassadine. 1981/Erik Hein

Eddie Albert, who starred on the popular 1960s sitcom *Green Acres*, originated the role of Jack Boland, a longtime friend and business acquaintance of Edward Quartermaine (John Ingle). When the writers decided to expand upon Jack, making him a longer-term role, Tim O'Connor, who had starred in the popular 1960s drama *Peyton Place*, took over.

Ron Reagan Jr. was cast as the manager of a massage parlor, giving the writers a chance to inject some political humor into the script. When Scotty Baldwin asked Reagan how much it would cost to use the phone, Reagan replied: "Ten bucks . . . twenty if you're a politician, could be thirty depending on which party." When Scotty noted that free enterprise was great, Reagan replied, "That's what my old man always says."

One of the more familiar faces in TV and in films through the years has been comedic actress Kathleen Freeman. Among her most notable roles was Sister Mary Stigmata in the 1980 Dan Ackroyd/John Belushi comedy *The Blues Brothers*. She was playing a nun once again when she turned up on *General Hospital* in 1991 as Sister Mary Dorothy, a friend of the Eckert family. In need of a disguise to elude the police, fugitive Mac Scorpio "borrowed" Sister Mary Dorothy's habit.

Esther Rolle, best known for her work in the 1970s sitcom *Good Times*, and Richard Roundtree, who had played Shaft in films and on television, had been real-life friends with the late Rosalind Cash, who played Mary Mae Ward. When Cash died and the producers decided to let the character of Mary Mae die as well rather than recast, Rolle and Roundtree sat among the mourners during the on-screen memorial service. Rolle and Roundtree, it should be noted, had previously worked on the soaps: *One Life to Live* and *Generations* respectively.

June Lockhart, best known for playing the mother on *Lassie* and on *Lost in Space*, first appeared as Felicia Jones's (Kristina Wagner) grandmother Maria Ramirez in 1984. Several times over the past thirteen years, she has returned to *General Hospital* for Felicia's weddings and varied crises.

As part of a cross-promotion between ABC's prime-time and daytime, Genie Francis and Tony Geary turned up in *Roseanne*'s diner as Luke and Laura. A few months later, Roseanne, along with her then husband Tom Arnold, returned the favor and journeyed into daytime. Roseanne played Jennifer Smith, the Mafia princess Luke had almost married back in 1980. The character, originated by Lisa Marie, had not been seen since shortly after the would-be wedding. Tom Arnold played Jennifer's husband, Billy "Bags" Bollman, a second-rate mobster who ran an Atlantic City casino with his wife. Luke and Laura fended off the aggressive advances of Jennifer and Billy while they searched for evidence that they could use against Jennifer's father, mobster Frank Smith (Mitchell Ryan).

Famous Fans
of the Show

*D*uring an airplane flight, actress/singer Julie Andrews once introduced herself to Norma Connolly, whom she recognized as Aunt Ruby.

Country singer Reba McEntire got hooked on *General Hospital* when she was only in the second grade. In the spring of 1997, she hosted the daytime miniseries *A Daytime to Remember*, introducing classic episodes from *General Hospital* as well as *One Life to Live* and *All My Children*.

Hockey player Wayne Gretzky checks into the soaps while working out in his home gym. He developed his liking for them when he was traveling around playing hockey with nothing to do in the afternoon but watch TV.

Atlanta Braves pitchers Kent Mercker and Steve Avery and catcher Gregg Olson paid a 1991 visit to the *General Hospital* set while in Los Angeles playing a baseball game. It was Olson's fourth trip to the set. Kansas City pitcher Bret Saberhagen once complained to *TV Guide* that the spring training schedule kept him from watching the show. And former New York Yankees outfielder Danny Tartabull was a big fan of Luke and Laura when they first got together.

Tennis superstar Chris Evert also got hooked on the Luke and Laura story line. According to her, she was not the only tennis player on the circuit tuning in.

Comedienne/actress Rosie O'Donnell, who has been watching the show since the 1970s, has brought several of the show's actors—among them Genie Francis and Tony Geary—onto her talk show.

Singer/songwriter Stevie Nicks, formerly of Fleetwood Mac, occasionally composes songs while watching *General Hospital*.

MacKenzie Phillips, who starred on the 1970s sitcom *One Day at a Time*, became a fan after the birth of her child.

Marla Maples Trump used to rush home from high school to watch *General Hospital* before rushing out again for basketball practice.

Andrew Stevens, who starred on *Dallas* and whose mother, Stella Stevens, would eventually work on *General Hospital*, once introduced himself to Sharon Wyatt and complimented her on her performance in the previous day's episode.

Actress Jean Simmons, who followed *General Hospital*, became a soap actress herself, landing a lead role in the prime-time revival of *Dark Shadows*.

The late Dame Judith Anderson, who was nominated for an Oscar for her work in the Hitchcock film *Rebecca*, continued to watch *General Hospital* even after she was cast on the rival soap *Santa Barbara*.

Mayim Bialik, who starred in the NBC sitcom *Blossom*, got to work with Finola Hughes (Anna Devane), who joined the show as her on-screen stepmother after leaving *General Hospital*.

The Artist Formerly Known as Prince cast Vanessa
Marcil (*Brenda Barrett*) in two videos, including "The
Most Beautiful Girl in the World," and later declared
Marcil the most beautiful girl in the world.

Actors Who Were Fans Before They Joined the Show

*L*ynn Herring (*Lucy Coe*) used to have a crush on Scotty Baldwin (Kin Shriner). After joining the show, she became one of Scotty's leading ladies.

Crystal Carson (ex–*Julia Barrett*) once had a crush on Luke Spencer (Tony Geary). She ended up as a love interest for Bill Eckert, who was also played by Tony Geary.

Nancy Grahn (*Alexa Davis*) was watching *General Hospital* during the Ice Princess adventure. Now she plays one of the villainous Cassadine clan that created the Ice Princess.

Leslie Horan (ex–*Miranda Jamison*) was watching back in the mid-'80s, when Frisco and Felicia (Jack and Kristina Wagner) were the show's top couple. After joining the show herself, Horan got to work with Kristina Wagner.

Joseph C. Phillips (*Justus Ward*) was a fan of the show back in his college days when Luke and Laura were the rage. From his very first day on the show, Phillips has been working extensively with both Genie Francis and Tony Geary.

Lieux Dressler (ex–*Alice Grant*) had been watching the show since its early days.

Robyn Bernard (ex–*Terry Brock*) first decided that she wanted to become an actress while watching General Hospital. A year after moving out to Los Angeles to pursue her dream, she landed a role on the show.

Cheryl Richardson (ex–*Jenny Eckert*) had been watching *General Hospital* since the mid-'70s and counted among her favorite story lines the one in which Lesley Webber (*Denise Alexander*) took the rap for a murder Laura had committed.

Edie Lehman (ex–*Katherine Delafield*) had also been watching the show during the mid to late '70s. She had stopped watching around the beginning of the Ice Princess adventure which, ironically enough, introduced her future leading man, Tristan Rogers, as Robert Scorpio.

Double Takes

*W*hen executive producer Gloria Monty returned to *General Hospital*, one of the first actors she lured back to the show was Tony Geary. Geary was willing to come back but wanted to try his hand at a new character. So the blue-collar family man Bill Eckert was created for him. Bill's resemblance to Luke Spencer was explained away in that they were cousins. In a move that unnerved many longtime fans, Bill went out on a date with Luke's sister Bobbie (Jacklyn Zeman). Fans had grown too accustomed to Geary and Zeman playing brother and sister to see them share a romantic kiss. When Luke agreed to reprise the role of Luke Spencer in 1993, the decision was made that Bill would be killed off. Luke and Bill shared two scenes together before the latter was gunned down by hit men hunting for Luke. "Bitter justice," Bill remarked as he died in Luke's arms, "the last face I see is my own."

Bill Eckert's last love interest before his death had been his cousin Luke's old flame, Holly Scorpio, played by Emma Samms. While involved with Holly, Bill and the audience learned that Holly had a look-alike half-sister named Paloma Perez, also played by Samms. Bill and Holly teamed up to rescue Paloma, a freedom fighter on the island nation of San Sebastian. Once the adventure story ended, Samms went back to playing just Holly.

In the mid-'80s, Kevin Bernhardt filled in as Frisco Jones during Jack Wagner's absence. Bernhardt impressed the producers enough that they rewarded him with the role of homicidal doctor Kevin O'Connor.

While Roy Thinnes originated the role of Jessie Brewer's two-timing husband Phil, a number of actors played the part after he left. Among them was Craig Huebing. In 1969, two years after he played Phil, Huebing returned to the show to take over the role of psychiatrist Peter Taylor, who fell in love with and married Phil's "widow," Jessie. That marriage was declared null and void when Phil Brewer turned up alive (played by Martin West). Robert Hogan, who had also played Phil briefly in the '60s, returned to the show later in a new role, that of Burt Marshall.

In 1986, John Ingle recurred on the show as an unnamed police commissioner. Seven years later, when David Lewis stepped down as Edward Quartermaine, Ingle was hired to take over the part.

In 1992, Leigh McCloskey was brought onto the show as Dr. Michael Baranski. Nothing much was done with the character, who quickly faded out of sight. A year later, McCloskey returned in a totally unrelated role as Mafia prince Damian Smith. This marked McCloskey's second time taking on a second role on the same soap. On *Santa Barbara,* he had played rapist Zach Kelton as well as distict attorney Ethan Asher.

Bradley Lockerman landed the most unusual role ever

cast on *General Hospital*, a space alien (named Casey) whom Robin Scorpio (Kimberly McCullough) befriended. Shortly after Casey returned to his home planet, Robin's mother Anna (Finola Hughes) was shocked to turn on the evening news and see reporter Shep Casey, who bore an unearthly resemblance to Casey the Alien. Aside from Anna's initial reaction, nothing was ever made of the resemblance between Casey the Alien and Shep Casey, the investigative reporter.

Henry Darrow, who would win an Emmy for his work on *Santa Barbara*, had several small roles on *General Hospital* over the years. Near the beginning of the show's run he played one of the lawyers handling Jessie Brewer's divorce from Phil Brent. In 1982, he played an ambassador, and five years later an army colonel working for the DVX.

In the mid-'80s, Brian Patrick Clarke joined the cast as Dr. Grant Putnam, who turned out to be a Russian spy by the name of André Chernin. The real Grant Putnam, who had been presumed dead, returned to town shortly after Putnam was exposed as an impostor. In an unexpected plot twist, the real Grant Putnam turned out to be a far worse threat than his impostor, who had since seen the error of his ways. The real Grant, who had killed his own brother, used his resemblance to the fake Grant to frame his impostor for attempted murder.

One of the more interesting evil twin story lines daytime has come up with has been that of Ryan Chamberlain and Kevin Collins, both played by Jon Lindstrom. When the character of Ryan arrived in Port Charles and stalked Felicia Jones (Kristina Wagner), no one—the audience included—knew he had a brother, let alone an identical twin. It wasn't until Ryan was shipped off to the mental

ABOVE Twin brothers Ryan Chamberlain and Kevin Collins (Jon Lindstrom) both stalked Felicia Jones (Kristina Wagner). 1996/Craig Sjodin/ABC OPPOSITE Also pictured: Lynn Herring (*Lucy Coe*). 1995/Wren Maloney

institution that Kevin showed up in town. Ryan managed to escape from the mental hospital twice and both times passed himself off as Kevin. What made this story line so interesting was that brother Kevin, a psychiatrist, was also mentally unbalanced. Haunted by his guilt over the incestuous abuse Ryan had suffered at the hands of their mother, Kevin eventually went off the deep end and resumed the reign of terror that Ryan had begun against Felicia years before.

Casting Stories

*E*die Lehman was not originally cast to play pianist Katherine Delafield—well, not all of her, at any rate. Lehman, a singer and musician, was hired simply to play the piano during close-up shots on Katherine's hands. Keely Shaye Smith, who has gone on to co-host *Unsolved Mysteries,* had been offered the role of Katherine. When the producers met Lehman, they decided that it would work out better and more cheaply for her to play all of Katherine, who was to be paired up romantically with spy turned police commissioner Robert Scorpio (Tristan Rogers). Keely Shaye Smith was subsequently hired on for a short-term role as Tony Jones's (Brad Maule) physical therapist.

Melbourne native Tristan Rogers had just about perfected his American accent when he was hired to play Australian secret agent Robert Scorpio. Chicago-born John J. York, on the other hand, had to create an Australian accent to try out for the role of Robert's younger brother Mac. He did so by studying language tapes and the Paul Hogan film *Crocodile Dundee.*

When the writers first conceived of the role of Anna

Devane, Robert Scorpio's never-before-mentioned wife, they envisioned the character as American. The British-born Finola Hughes so wowed the producers when she read for the part that the character was rewritten as British. Eventually, Hughes had to convince an even tougher audience that Anna should be British—namely the immigration department. In order to continue to work in the United States, Hughes and the show needed to prove that she brought something to the character that no American actress could.

As proof that not every future Hollywood star's potential is obvious from the beginning, Sharon Stone auditioned for a role on *General Hospital* in the late '70s. According to an interview she gave to *Vanity Fair,* the casting director told her that she had "no sense of mystery."

Judith Chapman, who had come close to landing the role of Pam Ewing on *Dallas,* impressed daytime producers and audiences alike with her mesmerizing portrayal of mystery woman Charlotte Greer on *Ryan's Hope. General Hospital* wanted Chapman so badly that they offered her a choice of two roles that were being introduced around the same time: spa owner Lorena Sharpe, who would be paired with Jimmy Lee Holt (Steve Bond) or Ginny Blake, who would turn out to be Mikey Webber's (David Mendenhall) biological mother. Chapman chose Ginny, and the role of Lorena went to Shelley Taylor Morgan. Five years later, on *Days of Our Lives,* Chapman would take over the role of Anjelica Deveraux from Shelley Taylor Morgan, who'd taken it over when Jane Elliot left *Days* to return to *General Hospital.*

In the mid-'80s, the character of singer Frisco Jones seemed like a star-making role for any aspiring singer/actor. *General Hospital,* the number one soap at the time, had helped along the musical career of Rick Springfield, who had never sung a note on the show. While Jack Wagner landed the role, a number of the other actors who auditioned for it wound up with roles connected to Frisco's story line. Brad Maule impressed the producers enough during his audition that the role of Frisco's brother Tony was created for him. Randall England was cast as Frisco's archenemy Jack Slater. And Kevin Berhnardt actually did get to play Frisco while Jack Wagner was out of work with a back injury. Although *Melrose Place*'s Grant Show did not win any roles on *General Hospital*, his audition for Frisco brought him to the attention of *Ryan's Hope*, where he worked for several years.

Several of the actors who auditioned for the role of A.J. Quartermaine wound up working on the show. Gerald Hopkins was hired to play A.J. in 1991, beating out Steve Burton, who was cast as A.J.'s brother Jason; Brandon Hooper, who was cast as Dr. Eric Simpson, a romantic rival of A.J.'s; and Sean Kanan, who eventually took over the role when the producers decided to take A.J. in a different direction.

Although Michael Sutton is several years older than Antonio Sabato Jr. (*Jagger Cates*), he was cast as Jagger's younger brother Stone.

Stephen Nichols (*Stefan Cassadine*) was first offered the role of Mafia prince Damian Smith, which would have reunited him with his *Days of Our Lives* leading lady Mary Beth Evans (*Katherine Bell*). Nichols turned the offer down to work on the short-lived prime-time serial *Second Chances* and to star in a film that never ended up being produced. Maurice Benard (*Sonny Corinthos*) was then offered his choice of roles—one being Damian, the other being Sonny. He picked Sonny because it was supposed to be short-term. Sonny, however, has survived Damian.

Originally, the producers only wanted Edie Lehman's (*Katherine Delafield*) hands. 1988/Daniel Watson/ABC

After being warned that the casting director thought that she was too attractive to play the role of mousy librarian Lucy Coe, Herring showed up at the interview wearing a high-collared blouse, ankle-length dress, the barest of makeup, and her hair pulled back into a tight bun. When she was brought in to meet producer Gloria Monty, she transformed from prim to sexy, letting her hair down and undoing a few buttons on her blouse. Not only did the transformation land Herring the job, it was re-created on screen in one of Herring's most memorable scenes.

Just as Crystal Carson was going in to audition for the role of Julia Barrett, the producers told her to forget about the script they had given her to memorize. They wanted her to wing her way through the scene. Since Tony Geary is famous for changing dialogue, they needed to see how quickly she thought on her feet. Although panic-stricken during the 5-4-3-2-1 countdown, as soon as the cameras started rolling, the words just came out of her mouth.

When Gloria Monty first met with Tony Geary about working on *General Hospital*, he told her flat out, "I hate soap operas." Monty responded, "So do I. I want you to help me change all that." Monty had recognized Geary's talents while directing him on the late '60s soap *Bright Promise* and had cast him in a movie of the week she did called *Sorority Kill*. The two of them discussed the idea of casting Geary as Mitch Williams, the corrupt district attorney, but neither liked him in that role, which went to Chris Pennock. With so many threatening letters aimed at Jacklyn Zeman for the trouble Bobbie was causing between Scotty and Laura (Kin Shriner and Genie Francis), Monty needed a character to take some of the heat away from Bobbie and Zeman herself. Monty solved both problems by creating for Geary the role of Bobbie's mob-connected brother Luke.

The Names Have Been Changed

*A*nna Lee (*Lila Quartermaine*) was born Joan Boniface Winnifrith. She chose the name Anna Lee from two books that she was reading: Tolstoy's *Anna Karenina* and a biography on Robert E. Lee.

Maurice Benard (*Sonny Corinthos*) anglicized his birth name after realizing that he was being typecast as Mauricio Morales. Benard was his grandmother's maiden name.

Steve Bond (ex–*Jimmy Lee Holt*) was born Shlomo Goldberg but changed it as a young actor to the more Hollywood-friendly Steve Bond at the insistence of his manager.

Kristina Wagner (*Felicia Jones*) went by the name Kristina Malandro until she married co-star Jack Wagner (ex–*Frisco Jones*).

Ron Hale (*Mike Corbin*) was born with the family name Thigpen.

Susan Pratt (ex–*Anne Logan*) joined the cast as Susan O'Hanlon but reverted back to her maiden name after her divorce.

Steve Bond's (*Jimmy Lee Holt*) agent didn't think he'd make it in Hollywood as Shlomo Goldberg. 1985/Erik Hein

Sam Behrens (ex–*Jake Meyer*) went by the name Stan Birnbaum when he was on *Ryan's Hope*.

Jack Betts (ex–*Dr. Ken Martin*) used the name Hunt Powers when he was on *General Hospital*.

Howard Sherman (ex–*Gordon Gray*) has flipped his name since his days on *General Hospital*.

Emma Samms (ex–*Holly Scorpio*) shortened her last

name from Samuelson to avoid charges of nepotism in her native England, where her father was a noted dancer.

Demi Moore (ex–*Jackie Templeton*), born Demetria Guynes, uses her ex–husband Freddy Moore's name and shortened her first name.

Rick Springfield (ex–*Dr. Noah Drake*) was born Richard Spring Thorpe. The last name Springfield has often gotten him confused with rock star Bruce Springsteen.

Carol Lawrence (ex–*Angela Eckert*) anglicized her Italian name, Carolina Maria Laraia, because people found it too long and hard to pronounce.

Gail Rae (ex–*Susan Moore*) added the last name Carlson to her own after marrying cast mate Steve Carlson (ex–*Gary Lansing*). Years later, after remarrying, she was using the last name Ramsey when she turned up on *Generations*.

Laura Harring (ex–*Carla Greco*) spelled her last name Herring when she appeared on *General Hospital*. She changed the *e* to an *a* to better reflect the correct pronunciation of the name. As it was, people tended to pronounce it the same as co-star Lynn Herring's name.

Janis Paige (*Aunt Iona Hutchison*) was born Donna Mae Jaden but changed it while making movies and starring on Broadway back in the 1940s.

Kurt Robin McKinney (ex–*Ned Ashton*) dropped his middle name after leaving *General Hospital* and turning up on *Guiding Light*.

Genie Francis (*Laura Spencer*) went by her full name, Genie Ann Francis, when she first appeared on the show.

Tuc Watkins (*Dr. Pierce Dorman*) was born Charles Curt Watkins III. When his parents tried to nickname him Curt, Watkins, who had a habit of speaking backwards as a child, turned Curt into Tuc, a nickname which then stuck. His agent tried to get him to add a *k* onto the end of *Tuc*. Watkins refused because the *T* looked a little too much like an *F*.

Tyler Baker (*Nikolas Cassadine*) recently dropped his last name and goes by his middle name, Christopher.

Mathew St. Patrick (*Marcus Taggert*) couldn't go by his real name, Patrick Mathew, because another actor in the union was using it. So he flipped his name and added in the "St." before Patrick in honor of his birthday, March 17.

Birthdays

January

1	Alexia Robinson (*Meg Lawson*)
2	Anna Lee (*Lila Quartermaine*)
7	Ron Hale (*Mike Corbin*)
16	Anders Hove (*Cesar Faison*)
17	Joseph C. Phillips (*Justus Ward*)
17	Jane Elliot (*Tracy Quartermaine*)
29	Matthew Ashford (*Tom Hardy*)

February

4	Stephanie Williams (*Simone Hardy*)
5	Stuart Damon (*Alan Quartermaine*)
11	Bianca Ferguson (*Claudia Phillips*)
13	Sharon Wyatt (*Tiffany Hill*)
15	Kurt Robin McKinney (*Ned Ashton*)
18	Sarah Brown (*Carly Roberts*)
19	Stephen Nichols (*Stefan Cassadine*)
22	Leslie Charleson (*Monica Quartermaine*)
26	Kevin Best (*Harrison Davis*)
27	Lieux Dressler (*Alice Grant*)
29	Antonio Sabato Jr. (*Jagger Cates*)

March

1	Maurice Benard (*Sonny Corinthos*)
5	Kimberly McCullough (*Robin Scorpio*)
6	Jacklyn Zeman (*Bobbie Jones*)
7	Glenn Walker Harris Jr. (*Sly Eckert*)
7	Mary Beth Evans (*Katherine Bell*)
9	Brad Lockerman (*Casey the Alien* and *Shep Casey*)
10	Senait Ashenafi (*Keesha Ward*)
17	Mathew St. Patrick (*Marcus Taggert*)

April

6	Roy Thinnes (*Phil Brewer*)
8	Bob Hastings (*Burt Ramsey*)
22	Steve Bond (*Jimmy Lee Holt*)
22	Ingo Rademacher (*Jasper Jax*)
27	Doug Sheehan (*Joe Kelly*)
28	Nancy Grahn (*Alexa Davis*)
29	Susan Pratt (*Anne Logan*)

May

4	Susan Brown (*Gail Baldwin*)
7	John Ingle (*Edward Quartermaine*)
8	Cheryl Richardson (*Jenny Eckert Hornsby*)
11	Jonathan Jackson (*Lucky Spencer*)
26	Robyn Bernard (*Terry Brock*)
26	Genie Francis (*Laura Spencer*)
29	Anthony Geary (*Luke Spencer*)

June

1	Robin Mattson (*Heather Webber*)
2	Maree Cheatham (*Charlene Simpson*)
3	Tristan Rogers (*Robert Scorpio*)
12	Felecia Bell (*Simone Hardy*)
18	Hugo Napier (*Larry Ashton*)
18	Michael Sutton (*Stone Cates*)

21	Leigh McCloskey (*Damian Smith*)
24	Crystal Carson (*Julia Barrett*)
28	Steve Burton (*Jason Quartermaine*)
29	Gail Rae Carlson (*Susan Moore*)

July

7	Vanita Harbour (*Dara Jensen*)
12	Gerald Gordon (*Dr. Mark Dante*)
17	Leslie Horan (*Miranda Jamison*)
18	Darlene Conley (*Trixie*)
24	Sam Behrens (*Jake Meyer*)
26	Nicholas Walker (*Jimmy O'Herlihy*)
30	Lilly Melgar (*Lily Rivera*)
31	Gerald Anthony (*Marco Dane*)
31	Wally Kurth (*Ned Ashton*)

August

1	Brian Patrick Clarke (*Grant Putnam*)
19	John Stamos (*Blackie Parrish*)
19	Paul Satterfield Jr. (*Paul Hornsby*)
20	Norma Connolly (*Ruby Anderson*)
23	Rick Springfield (*Noah Drake*)
28	Emma Samms (*Holly Scorpio*)

September

2	Tuc Watkins (*Dr. Pierce Dorman*)
5	Cari Shayne (*Karen Wexler Cates*)
15	Scott Thompson Baker (*Colton Shore*)
19	Tonja Walker (*Olivia Jerome*)
22	Lynn Herring (*Lucy Coe*)
23	Shell Danielson (*Dominique Baldwin*)
25	Edie Lehman (*Katherine Delafield*)
25	Todd Davis (*Bryan Phillips*)

October

3	Jack Wagner (*Frisco Jones*)
5	Shell Kepler (*Amy Vining*)
15	Vanessa Marcil (*Brenda Barrett*)
18	Jon Lindstrom (*Kevin Collins*)
19	David Lewis (*Edward Quartermaine*)
29	Finola Hughes (*Anna Lavery*)
30	Kristina Wagner (*Felicia Jones*)

November

2	Rachel Ames (*Audrey Hardy*)
2	Sean Kanan (*A.J. Quartermaine*)
5	Jennifer Guthrie (*Dawn Winthrop*)
5	Chris Robinson (*Rick Webber*)
10	Loanne Bishop (*Rose Kelly*)
11	Demi Moore (*Jackie Templeton*)
11	John Reilly (*Sean Donely*)
11	Denise Alexander (*Lesley Webber*)
17	Frank Maxwell (*Dan Rooney*)
23	David Wallace (*Tom Hardy*)
30	Sherilyn Wolter (*Celia Quartermaine*)

December

2	Rena Sofer (*Lois Cerullo Ashton*)
5	Peter Hansen (*Lee Baldwin*)
6	Kin Shriner (*Scotty Baldwin*)
10	John J. York (*Mac Scorpio*)
24	Ricky Martin (*Miguel Morez*)

Relatively Speaking

*N*oting the physical similarity between Sean Kanan and Steve Burton, who play half-brothers A.J. Quartermaine and Jason Morgan, many fans have written in to soap magazines asking if the two are related in real life. As it turns out, the two are cousins—but only by marriage.

John Travolta's sister Ellen Travolta has recurred on *General Hospital* over the past few years as Gloria Cerullo, mother to Lois Cerullo Ashton (Rena Sofer).

Cher's sister Georgeann LaPiere originated the role of Heather Grant Webber.

Amber Tamblyn's (*Emily Quartermaine*) father Russ Tamblyn appeared in the 1960s movie musical *West Side Story* and in the prime-time soap opera *Twin Peaks*. He danced on *General Hospital* with his daughter during the 1997 Nurses' Ball.

Anna Lee's (*Lila Quartermaine*) son Jeffrey Byron is a soap actor himself, who has played Richard Abbott on *One Life to Live* and Dr. Jeff Martin on *All My Children*.

Producer Gloria Monty hired her sister Norma as the show's head writer.

Ian Buchanan, who originated the role of Duke Lavery, is descended from Scottish poet Robert Burns.

John Travolta's sister Ellen (*Gloria Cerullo*) played mother to Rena Sofer (*Lois Cerullo Ashton*), seen here with Wally Kurth (*Ned Ashton*). 1995/Craig Sjodin/ABC

Gregory Beecroft, who took over the role of Duke Lavery, is the brother of David Beecroft, who played Trent Chapin on *One Life to Live* and Nick Agretti on *Falcon Crest*.

Rick Moses, who played redeemed hit man Hutch, is the brother of Billy Moses, who has worked on the prime-time serials *Falcon Crest* and *Melrose Place*.

Bob Hastings's (ex-*Burt Ramsey*) brother Don Hastings has been playing Dr. Bob Hughes on *As the World Turns* for the past thirty-seven years.

Family and *Empty Nest* star Kristy McNichol's brother, James McNichol, played bellhop/songwriter Josh Clayton.

Rachel Ames's (*Audrey Hardy*) mother, Dorothy

Adams, made close to forty films, among them *Laura* and *The Ten Commandments*. Ames's father, actor Byron Foulger, worked on the '60s sitcom *Petticoat Junction* and appeared in some two hundred films, including *The Lost Weekend, Pocketful of Miracles,* and *The Postman Always Rings Twice*. On *General Hospital*, he played the minister who married Steve and Audrey.

Monkee Mickey Dolenz's daughter Amy Dolenz played late-'80s teen-heroine Melissa McKee.

Kin Shriner's (*Scotty Baldwin*) father was famed humorist Herb Shriner and his brother is comedian/former talk show host Will Shriner, who appeared on *General Hospital* as an extra at Scotty's wedding to Laura and as himself in a segment where cosmetics executive Scotty appeared on ABC's *Home Show*.

Wings star Crystal Bernard's sister Robyn Bernard played Terry Brock.

Beverlee McKinsey, who became one of daytime's premiere actresses for her work on *Another World* in the '70s and *Guiding Light* in the '80s and '90s, appeared on *General Hospital* as Myrna Slaughter, a former film star who testified at Edward Quartermaine's murder trial. McKinsey's son Scott is one of the directors on the show.

Clark Gable and Loretta Young's daughter, Judy Lewis, played Barbara Vining, the woman who raised Laura Spencer.

Genie Francis (*Laura Spencer*) is the daughter of character actor Ivor Francis, who played Professor Mitchell on *Bright Promise* and guested as a doctor on *General Hospital*.

The Mount Rushmore location shoot had to be taped in three days because of an impending directors' strike. Pictured here: Robyn Bernard (*Terry Brock*) and Shaun Cassidy (*Dusty Walker*). 1987/Jerry Fitzgerald

Real-Life Romances

*O*ver the past couple of year's Wally Kurth's life has been closely parallelling his storyline as Ned Ashton. Like Kurth, Ned has been moonlighting as a rock-and-roll singer. And, just as Ned fell in love with Lois Cerullo and married her in secret, Kurth fell for Rena Sofer and married her without letting the press know that they were even engaged. Sofer's real-life pregnancy was then written into Lois's story line.

Genie Francis is married to *Star Trek: The Next Generation*'s Jonathan Frakes, whom she met while working on the prime-time serial *Bare Essence*. They fell in love while working together on the miniseries *North and South*. The two made a brief appearance together in *Camp Nowhere*, playing parents to Francis's *GH* son Jonathan Jackson (*Lucky Spencer*).

One of the most popular couples on the show during the '80s was Frisco and Felicia, played by Jack Wagner and Kristina Malandro, who fell in love with each other in real life. When they married in December 1993, Malandro took her husband's name, a rare move for an actress with an established career. Each of Malandro's pregnancies was

Felicia and Frisco, flanked here by Robin (Kimberly McCullough) and Tony (Brad Maule), married twice before their real-life counterparts, Jack Wagner and Kristina Malandro, made it to the altar. 1986/Craig Sjodin/ABC

written into Frisco and Felicia's story lines with one notable exception: While Malandro has given birth to two boys, Felicia has given birth to two girls.

Lynn Herring is married to Wayne Northrop, whom she met in acting class. They have been married since 1981. In 1992, she worked with Northrop briefly on *Days of Our Lives*, where he played detective Roman Brady. He and Herring currently work together on *Port Charles*.

Herring's leading man John Lindstrom has his own connection to *Days of Our Lives*. He is married to Eileen Davidson, who plays Kristen Blake on the show.

Rachel Ames is married to actor Barry Cahill, with whom she worked on the 1969 feature film *Daddy's Gone a Huntin'*.

Norma Connolly was married for more than twenty years to screenwriter Howard Rodman, who co-scripted such films as *Coogan's Bluff* and *Charley Varrick*.

Nancy Grahn once dated former *General Hospital* leading man Sam Behrens (*Jake Meyer*). On their first date, Behrens, a recently licensed pilot, took her flying.

Jacklyn Zeman was once married to the late disc jockey Murray "the K" Kaufman, who was once nicknamed "The Fifth Beatle." She is currently married to real estate developer Glenn Gorden.

Anna Lee (*Lila Quartermaine*) was married for ten years to director Robert Stevenson, who worked with her in a number of films during the '40s and was later nominated for an Oscar for directing the Disney classic *Mary Poppins*. Lee later married the late writer Robert Nathan, best known for his novels *Portrait of Jennie* and *The Bishop's Wife*.

Jane Elliot was once married to *General Hospital* cameraman Luis Rojas.

Vanita Harbour (*Dara Jensen*) is married to Allan Dean Moore, who played her leading man on *One Life to Live*.

Quick Facts About the Stars

Family

Tony Geary's (*Luke Spencer*) aunt used to introduce him as "my nephew, Luke Spencer."

Brad Maule's (*Dr. Tony Jones*) sister Linda works for the CIA.

Chris Robinson (*Rick Webber*) adopted a young fan of the show who had lost his father.

Matthew Ashford (*Dr. Tom Hardy*) grew up the fifth of eight children.

Sharon Wyatt (*Tiffany Hill*) grew up in the same town of Carthage, Tennessee, as Vice President Al Gore, who was friends with her older brother. During the 1992 presidential election, Wyatt slipped a reference to Gore into her dialogue, referring to him as "my man from Carthage."

Stuart Damon's (*Dr. Alan Quartermaine*) parents escaped from Russia during the Bolshevik Revolution.

In toy stores, Sarah Brown's (*Carly Roberts*) father points to the Pink Ranger doll from the *V.R. Troopers* series she starred in and lets people know that she's his daughter.

The Press

Kristina Wagner (*Felicia Jones*), Antonio Sabato Jr. (*Jagger Cates*), and Vanessa Marcil (*Brenda Barrett*) have all been picked as *People* magazine's 50 Most Beautiful People in the World.

Nude photos of Steve Bond (*Jimmy Lee Holt*) that had been taken early in his career resurfaced for *Playgirl* after he landed his role on *General Hospital*.

Emma Samms (*Holly Sutton*) had been approached twice by *Playboy* to be the centerfold but turned the magazine down both times.

Genie Francis (*Laura Spencer*), Robin Mattson (*Heather Webber*), and Jacklyn Zeman (*Bobbie Spencer*) posed with their clothes *on* for a 1982 *Playboy* pictorial saluting the women of daytime television.

In addition to acting, Emma Samms is a professional photographer whose work has appeared in such prestigious magazines as *Architectural Digest.*

Genie Francis was the first soap actress featured on the cover of *TV Guide*. She and Tony Geary are the only two daytime soap stars to make the cover of *People* magazine twice. They also appeared on the cover of *Newsweek.*

Matthew Ashford was named Most Hated Man on Daytime TV by *Soap Opera Digest* while he was working on *Days of Our Lives.*

Education

John Ingle (*Edward Quartermaine*) founded the performing arts departments at both Hollywood and Beverly Hills High Schools and taught such future stars as Albert Brooks, Nicolas Cage, Richard Dreyfuss, Joanna Gleason,

Barbara Hershey, Swoosie Kurtz, Stefanie Powers, David Schwimmer, and Jonathan Silverman.

Emma Samms earned a certificate as an emergency medical technician and subscribes to a number of medical journals.

Brooke Bundy (*Diana Taylor*) was Steve Burton's (*Jason Morgan*) first acting teacher.

Norma Connolly (*Ruby Spencer*) helped set up a scholarship in memory of her good friend, sitcom star Donna Reed.

Lynn Herring (*Lucy Coe*) has a degree in psychology from Louisiana State University.

Stuart Damon has a degree in psychology from Brandeis University and originally intended to pursue a career in law.

Joseph Phillips (*Justus Ward*) considered a career in law and was accepted to Rutgers University in 1993, one year before he began playing lawyer Justus Ward.

Emma Samms had studied ballet, but a case of bursitis ended her dreams of becoming a dancer at age 16.

Sean Kanan (*A.J. Quartermaine*) has taught Steve Burton how to follow the stock market.

Ingo Rademacher (*Jasper Jacks*) studied forestry in college.

Honors

Anna Lee (*Lila Quartermaine*) was made an Honorary Private in the Sixth Army by General George Patton himself for her volunteer work with the U.S.O. during World War II.

In 1982, Queen Elizabeth presented Anna Lee the M.B.E. (Member of the Order of the British Empire).

In 1964, *Theatre World* named Stuart Damon the Most Promising Performer of the Year for his performance in *The Boys From Syracuse*.

Lynn Herring was named Miss Virginia 1977 and was a runner-up in the 1978 Miss USA pageant. Laura Herring

(*Carla Greco*) was chosen Miss USA in 1985. Tonja Walker (*Olivia Jerome*), the 1979 Miss Teen All American, represented Miss Maryland in the 1980 Miss USA pageant and was one of the ten finalists.

Both Anna Lee and John Beradino (*Dr. Steve Hardy*) got their Stars on Hollywood's Walk of Fame in 1993.

Sports

John Beradino played second base for the Cleveland Indians, who won the 1948 World Series. Thirty-plus years later, he appeared in the TV movie *Don't Look Back* about his former Indians teammate Satchel Paige, the first black pitcher in baseball. A leg injury ended Beradino's professional baseball career.

As a publicity stunt, the St. Louis Browns' team owner insured John Beradino's face for a million dollars.

Brad Lockerman (*Casey the Alien* and *Shep Casey*) broke his shoulder in a motorcycle accident the night before he was to try out with the Pittsburgh Pirates baseball team.

During his teens, Steve Bond competed in the professional rodeo circuit. His rodeo days ended when a bull fell on him.

Leslie Charleson (*Dr. Monica Quartermaine*) owns an Andalusian horse named Andarra whom she enters in horse shows.

Sean Kanan began karate and kick-boxing lessons when he was thirteen, skills that helped land him a co-starring role opposite Ralph Macchio in the third *Karate Kid* movie.

Brian Patrick Clarke (*Grant Andrews* and *Grant Putnam*) played pro football with the Memphis Southmen of the World Football League but was cut midway through his first season.

Ingo Rademacher was a ski champion at the age of eight.

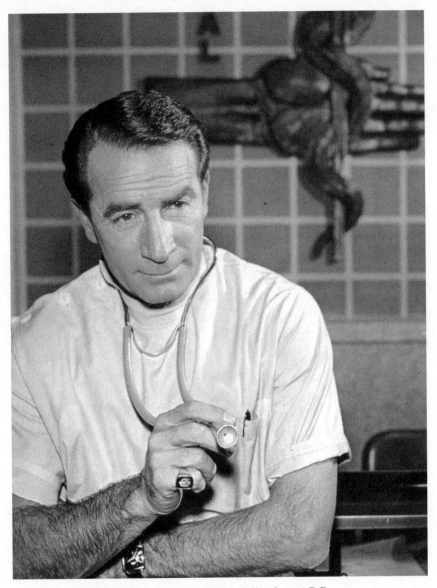

John Beradino's (*Steve Hardy*) million-dollar face. ABC

Brandon Hooper (*Dr. Eric Simpson*) competed on the Junior Olympic ski team.

Jack Wagner (*Frisco Jones*) is a pro-level golfer.

Big Breaks

Kimberly McCullough (*Robin Scorpio*) made her show business debut at the age of seven months, when she appeared in a diaper commercial with Juliet Mills.

Tony Geary was discovered by Jack Albertson (*Chico and the Man*).

Genie Francis made her acting debut on the prime-time drama *Family*.

John Beradino began his show business career as a child, working as an extra in the *Our Gang* comedies.

Denise Alexander (*Dr. Lesley Webber*) began her show business career at the age of five, working on radio soaps.

Scott Thompson Baker (*Colton Shore*) won the Grand First Prize in the acting category on *Star Search*. His future leading lady Laura Herring represented Mexico and became a champion on an international edition of *Star Search*.

Jon Lindstrom (*Ryan Chamberlain* and *Kevin Collins*) was discovered while tending bar at Morton's restaurant. Producer Steve Tisch, whose office was next door to the restaurant, offered him a job playing a waiter on the ABC drama *Call to Glory*. Tisch later offered him a role on the syndicated soap opera *Rituals*.

Guy Mack (*Dr. Patrick O'Connor*) was also discovered while busing tables at Morton's by John Crosby, who worked in the ABC development program.

Names

Producer Shelly Curtis was a former student of John Ingle. As such, she has a hard time calling him by his first name.

Senait Ashenafi (*Keesha Ward*) prefers to go by her first

Jon Lindstrom (*Ryan Chamberlain* and *Kevin Collins*) was discovered while tending bar. 1995/Wren Maloney

Rosalind Cash (*Mary May Ward*) was named after the Shakespearean heroine. 1995 Mitchell Haaseth/ABC

name because people find her last name so difficult to pronounce. Her first name means "peaceful one."

Days of Our Lives star Jason Brooks gave Sean Kanan the nickname Rudy after a soap opera–themed *Family Feud* tournament where Sean answered "Rudyard Kipling" when asked to name a famous British person.

Ingo Rademacher's last name means "wheel maker."

Rosalind Cash (*Mary Mae Ward*) was named after the heroine in Shakespeare's *As You Like It.*

Wally Kurth and Rena Sofer (*Ned* and *Lois Ashton*) gave their baby daughter the middle name Rosalind in honor of the late Rosalind Cash.

Sarah Brown's agents suggested that she change her name to something more Hollywood, but Brown refused.

Soap Actors Playing Soap Actors

Emma Samms played a soap actress in the John Candy comedy *Delirious.*

Matthew Ashford played a soap opera actor on the sci-fi series *Quantum Leap.*

Stuart Damon and Robin Mattson played soap actors in the TV movie *Fantasies.*

The last Perry Mason movie starring Raymond Burr, *The Case of the Killer Kiss,* starred three actors from *General Hospital:* Sean Kanan, Stuart Damon, and Genie Francis.

Finola Hughes (*Anna Devane*) and Stephen Nichols (*Stefan Cassadine*) did cameos as soap actors in the big-screen soap spoof *Soapdish.* Nichols also played a soap actor on an episode of the CBS sitcom *The Nanny.*

Lynn Herring played herself in the TV movie of Deidre Hall's surrogate motherhood, *Never Say Never: The Deidre Hall Story.*

Other Notable TV and Film Roles

Vanessa Marcil played Nicolas Cage's girlfriend in the action film *The Rock*, one of the five biggest grossing movies of 1996.

Justin Cooper (*Lucas Jones*) played Jim Carrey's son in the 1997 blockbuster comedy *Liar Liar*.

David Lewis (*Edward Quartermaine*) recurred as Warden Crichton on the '60s live-action *Batman* series. John Ingle's scene as Batman's doctor was cut from *Batman Forever*.

John Beradino was a guest star on *Superman* in the 1950s and *Batman* in the 1960s.

Jane Elliot (*Tracy Quartermaine*) played a nun in the Mary Tyler Moore/Elvis Presley film *A Change of Habit*.

Australian-born Tristan Rogers (*Robert Scorpio*) provided the voice for Jake, a kangaroo mouse, in the Disney animated film *The Rescuers Down Under*.

Tuc Watkins (*Dr. Pierce Dorman*) was cut from his very first acting job, an under-five role as a gym attendant on the ABC sitcom *Growing Pains*.

As a child, Steve Bond played Boy in *Tarzan and the Jungle Boy*. Ingo Rademacher almost landed the title role in the current syndicated *Tarzan* series.

Tony Geary appeared in one of the very first episodes of *All in the Family*. He played a friend of Mike's whom Archie mistakenly thinks is gay. In the same episode Phil Carey (*Asa Buchanan*, *One Life to Live*) plays an ex-football player/drinking buddy of Archie's who Mike learns is gay.

Anders Hove (*Cesar Faison*) and Michael Watson (*Decker Moss*) played half-brothers in the horror film *Subspecies*—one a vampire, the other a human.

John Ingle has been kissed by Cindy Crawford in two different commercials for Revlon lipstick.

Maurice Benard (*Sonny Corinthos*) played Desi Arnaz in the TV movie *Lucy and Desi: Before the Laughter.*

Genie Francis played Jessica Fletcher's (Angela Lansbury) niece in two episodes of *Murder She Wrote*.

Tristan Rogers was paired with *All My Children*'s Susan Lucci on an episode of *The Love Boat*. Chris Robinson played Lucci's husband on an episode of *Fantasy Island*.

Sarah Brown landed the role of the Pink Ranger in *V.R. Troopers* on her nineteenth birthday.

Director Mike Nichols hired Leslie Charleson for a role in *Day of the Dolphin* after spotting her in a commercial for tooth polish.

Lynn Herring performed a high-wire act on *Circus of the Stars*.

Chris Robinson originated the "I'm not a doctor but I play one on TV" commercial.

Other Jobs

Tony Geary once sold toys in a department store.

Sharon Wyatt sold cemetery plots.

Before becoming an actor, John Reilly (*Sean Donely*) had worked for ten years as a business executive in a packaging firm.

Sean Kanan performs stand-up comedy and can do a number of impersonations, including Jack Nicholson and Clint Eastwood.

Shelley Taylor Morgan (*Lorena Sharpe*) went on to host the soap opera talk show *Pure Soap* on E!

During the early '50s, Anna Lee was a panelist on the

quiz show *It's News to Me*, which was hosted in its final season by Walter Cronkite.

Susan Brown (*Dr. Gail Baldwin*) runs her own design business. One of her clients has been cast mate Leslie Charleson, whose bathroom, bedroom, and den Brown has redesigned.

In 1994, Vanessa Marcil was the first regular host for the late-night music series *In Concert*.

Judith Chapman (*Ginny Blake*) has opened a restaurant in Palm Springs.

Senait Ashenafi worked briefly as a model on the game show *The Price Is Right*.

Shell Kepler (*Amy Vining*) has designed and sold more than $20 million worth of clothing on the Home Shopping Network under the label Lacey Afternoon. She also designed a line of clothing for JCPenney, which she called Simply Shell.

Denise Alexander produced the Lifetime film *Hidden in Silence*. She is currently working on a children's book.

Don Galloway (*Dr. Buzz Stryker*) now works as a police officer.

Emily McLaughlin (*Jessie Brewer*) wrote lyrics for songs composed by her husband Jeffrey Hunter.

Animals

The dog that plays Lila Quartermaine's Annabelle is actually named Treasure, while Lucky Spencer's Foster is named Foster in real life as well.

Finola Hughes played Victoria, the White Cat, in the original London production of Andrew Lloyd Webber's long-running musical *Cats*.

Wally Kurth named his dog Sally after Sally Field.

Rena Sofer owned a five-foot-long boa constrictor as a pet. She named it Yael (meaning "from God").

Maurice Benard named one of his dogs Nico after the character he played on *All My Children*.

Back when she was directing *The Secret Storm* in the 1950s, Gloria Monty was once chased down the hallway by a cow that had escaped from the nearby *Captain Kangaroo* set.

Celebrity Encounters

Leigh McCloskey (*Damian Smith*) roomed with *Frasier* star Kelsey Grammer while attending the Juilliard school.

Senait Ashenafi originally moved to Los Angeles with the intention of becoming a singer. She appeared in the video for Michael Jackson's "Remember the Time."

While Felecia Bell (*Dr. Simone Hardy*) was modeling in Japan, rock star Sting walked up to her in a nightclub to tell her that she had "the greatest legs in Tokyo." She taught him to do the Cabbage Patch dance.

Stuart Damon danced in the chorus line of the Broadway musical *Irma La Douce* alongside future film star Elliott Gould.

Ian Buchanan (*Duke Lavery*) landed the role of Ian during the last season of *It's Garry Shandling's Show* after meeting Shandling in the parking lot outside the *General Hospital* studio. (*General Hospital* and *It's Garry Shandling's Show* were shot in adjacent studios.) After a few conversations, Shandling decided that he liked Buchanan's sense of humor and invited him to appear on the show. Buchanan balanced the two shows, doing *General Hospital* in the morning and *Garry Shandling* in the afternoon.

On Anna Lee's first night in America, David O. Selznik invited her and her husband, director Robert Stevenson, to view a rough cut of *Gone With the Wind* with him, Clark Gable, and Carole Lombard.

Crystal Carson (*Julia Barrett*) played one of Madonna's bridesmaids in *Who's That Girl?* On the third day of filming, Carson met Madonna during an early morning taping. Madonna walked up to her and said, "We don't look so pretty at four in the morning, do we?" Carson replied, "I wouldn't talk. You look like shit." After that, the two of them got along beautifully.

Miscellaneous Facts

Stephen Nichols once considered becoming a monk.

Vanessa Marcil has been a vegetarian since birth and has never eaten meat.

When the riots broke out in Los Angeles following the Rodney King verdict, Anna Lee stationed herself in her front hallway with a shotgun in case the trouble reached her house.

Norma Connolly has served as vice president for the Screen Actors Guild.

While working on the Brooklyn-taped soap *Another World*, Denise Alexander shuttled between New York and Los Angeles on a weekly basis.

Kristina Wagner's personal manager is Elissa Leeds (*Steffi Brewster*), who played Jack Wagner's first love interest on *General Hospital*.

Ingo Rademacher is a certified lifeguard.

Tony Geary turned fifty years old in 1997.

Anna Lee's license plate used to read LILA Q.

Lilly Melgar (*Lily Rivera Corinthos*), Anna Lee, and Sarah Brown's homes have all gone up in flames in the last few years.

Foreign Soil

Match up each of the following actors with the country in which he or she was born. As you will note, not all of the foreign-born stars are easily recognized as such. Some answers may be used two or more times. (Answers on page 194.)

1. Anna Lee (*Lila Quartermaine*)
2. Tristan Rogers (*Robert Scorpio*)
3. Emma Samms (*Holly Sutton*)
4. Steve Bond (*Jimmy Lee Holt*)
5. Finola Hughes (*Anna Devane*)
6. Ian Buchanan (*Duke Lavery*)
7. Senait Ashenafi (*Keesha Ward*)
8. Anders Hove (*Cesar Faison*)
9. Laura Herring (*Carla Greco*)
10. Ingo Rademacher (*Jasper Jax*)
11. Réal Andrews (*Taggert*)
12. Antonio Sabato Jr. (*Jagger Cates*)

a. Australia
b. Scotland
c. Canada
d. Denmark
e. Ethiopia
f. England
g. Germany
h. Israel
i. Italy
j. Mexico

Jax hails from down under, but was Ingo Rademacher born there as well? Also pictured: Vanessa Marcil (*Brenda*) and Maurice Benard (*Sonny*). 1996/Craig Sjodin/ABC

From Salem to Port Charles

*S*ince the arrival of supervising producer Shelley Curtis, who used to work on *Days of Our Lives*, a number of that show's most popular and talented alumni have been turning up in Port Charles. But the trend, as you will see, did not begin with Curtis.

Denise Alexander (*Lesley Webber*) had played *Days of Our Lives*'s emotionally troubled Susan Hunter from 1966 to 1973. In a plotline similar to one her on-screen daughter Laura would go through on *General Hospital*, Susan claimed to have been raped by a man she encountered in the park, then later realized with the help of therapy that she had entered into willing sexual relations with him. *General Hospital* lured fan favorite Alexander away from *Days* with what was then estimated to be the highest salary earned by a daytime performer.

Mary Beth Evans and Stephen Nichols (*Katherine Bell* and *Stefan Casadine*) had become one of *Days* and daytime's most popular couples as nurse Kayla Brady and reformed thug Patch during the '80s. They have recently been recoupled on *General Hospital*, but with one notable

General Hospital reunited Mary Beth Evans (*Katherine Bell*) with former leading man Stephen Nichols (*Stefan Cassadine*). 1997/Cathy Blaivas/ABC

alteration: Katherine is not quite the Girl Scout that Kayla was. Matthew Ashford (*Tom Hardy*) had worked extensively with Evans and Nichols on *Days* as well. He played Patch's long-lost brother Jack Deveraux, who married and raped Kayla when he realized that she still loved Patch.

Playing Jack's adoptive mother Anjelica Deveraux was Jane Elliot (*Tracy Quartermaine*). Among the men Anjelica bedded was Justin Kiriakis, played by Wally Kurth, who eventually took over the role of Tracy's son Ned. For fans of both shows, the casting of Kurth as Elliot's on-screen son added a stronger hint of incest to a character who had already slept with his aunt by marriage, Monica.

Like Jane Elliot, Genie Francis had stopped over in

Salem for several years in between her stints on *General Hospital*. As newspaper reporter Diana Colville, she was paired with the show's leading man Drake Hogestyn (a *Roman Brady* impostor) and ended up in a series of Luke and Laura–styled romantic adventures all across the globe.

Steve Burton had a small, recurring role as Michael Harris on *Days* before signing on as *General Hospital*'s Jason Quartermaine.

Lynn Herring (*Lucy Coe*) specifically left *General Hospital* in early 1992 for *Days,* where her husband Wayne Northrop played the real Roman Brady. Herring, who played lawyer Lisanne Gardner, only got to do a couple of scenes with Northrop, including one where Roman, working undercover as a cleaning lady, emptied a vacuum cleaner bag onto her head. The role of Lisanne proved short-lived, and Herring was back on *General Hospital* by the end of the year.

Billy Warlock won the 1987 Daytime Emmy as Best Young Actor for his role as *Days* teen hero Frankie Brady. Ten years later, he took over the role of A.J. Quartermaine.

Distinguished Alumni

*H*ollywood's highest paid actress Demi Moore—who has starred in blockbusters such as *Ghost, Indecent Proposal,* and *Disclosure*—played investigative reporter Jackie Templeton on *General Hospital* from 1982–83. From her first day, she seemed destined for stardom. Her first month on the show, *US* magazine put her on its cover alongside Tony Geary (*Luke Spencer*). Although intended as a love interest for Luke, Jackie ended up with his best friend, Robert Scorpio (*Tristan Rogers*).

Moore shared an early scene with future Academy Award nominee Sally Kirkland (*Anna*), who did a day stint on the show as a prostitute. Kirkland later landed a lead role in the short-lived late-night soap *Valley of the Dolls.*

Playing Jackie Templeton's sister Laura was Janine Turner, who has gone on to star in the TV series *Northern Exposure* as well as in films such as the Sylvester Stallone action flick *Cliffhanger.* Wearing her hair longer and dyed blond, Turner was a dead ringer for Genie Francis. The resemblance was integral to the story line in which Laura Spencer was kidnapped and presumably killed by David Gray (Paul Rossilli), who thought he was stalking Laura Templeton.

Future movie stars Janine Turner and Demi Moore played sisters
Laura and Jackie Templeton in the early '80s. 1983/Erik Hein

Among Janine Turner's leading men during her two years on the show was John Stamos, who played reformed street tough Blackie Parrish. After Blackie was sent to jail for killing his girlfriend, Stamos tried his hand in prime-time. After two short-lived sitcoms, *Dreams* and *You Again* with Jack Klugman, he landed the role of Uncle Jessie in the long-running ABC sitcom *Full House*. In the episode where his character Jessie got married, Stamos's good friend and former *General Hospital* cast mate Kin Shriner (*Scotty Baldwin*) played a police officer. Not forgetting the fact that *General Hospital* launched his career, Stamos later returned to the show for one episode as himself in a scene that featured Shriner as Scotty.

Although Scotty Baldwin was played longest and most memorably by Kin Shriner, the role was originated in 1965 by child actor Johnnie Whittaker, who would go on to star as Jodie in *Family Affair* and as Sigmund in *Sigmund and the Sea Monsters* on TV as well as such children's films as *Moreover and Me*.

Justin Whalin, who took over the role of Jimmy Olsen in the Superman-based prime-time series *Lois and Clark*, played a teen-aged A.J. Quartermaine in the late '80s. (Sean Kanan, who currently plays A.J., guest-starred on *Lois and Clark* during the 1995–96 season.) On the *Superboy* series of the early '90s, Howard Sherman, who originated the role of Laura Webber's biological father Gordon Gray, played archenemy Lex Luthor.

Richard Dean Anderson left his role as Dr. Jeff Webber in 1981 as the show started to shift from medical drama to action adventure. Ironically, Anderson is now best known as the title hero for his role in the 1980s action adventure *MacGyver*, which ran on ABC from 1985–92.

In the late '70s, when Lesley Webber (Denise Alexander)

Before *MacGyver*, Richard Dean Anderson, pictured here with Susan Pratt (*Anne Logan*), played Dr. Jeff Webber from 1976–81. 1980/ABC

was having problems with husband Rick Webber (Chris Robinson), she joined a counseling group that also included garage mechanic Spence Andrews, played by future *Hill Street Blues* star Daniel J. Travanti. (Spence's estranged wife Jonelle was played by former Miss America Mary Ann Mobley.) Spence fell for Lesley, but she didn't return his affection. Travanti's *Hill Street Blues* co-star James B. Sikking had played alcoholic cardiac surgeon Dr. James Hobart on *General Hospital* during the mid-'70s.

Before starring as Luke Skywalker in the *Star Wars* trilogy, Mark Hamill had played Jessie Brewer's (Emily McLaughlin) troubled nephew Kent Murray. Leonard Nimoy, who starred in the *Star Trek* TV and film series, worked for a few days during *General Hospital*'s early years as a drug dealer named Benny. Roy Thinnes, who originated the role of Jessie's cheating husband, Dr. Phil Brewer, went on to star on the 1960s cult sci-fi series *The Invaders*.

Ed Platt, who played the chief on the 1960s spy spoof *Get Smart*, worked on *General Hospital* during the show's first year as Dr. Miller. Also featured on the show during those early days was former matinee idol Neil Hamilton (as Philip Mercer), who would go on to play Commissioner Gordon on the live action *Batman* series of the '60s.

Former *Saturday Night Live* regular Victoria Jackson did day work on the show back in the early '80s.

Antonio Sabato Jr., who played Jagger Cates for two years in the early '90s, has gained prominence as the latest underwear model for Calvin Klein. He has also starred in the short-lived sci-fi series *Earth 2* and guested for six episodes on *Melrose Place* as Amanda Woodard's (Heather Locklear) abusive ex-husband Jack Parezi. His father was played by David Groh, who had played Bobbie Spencer's (Jacklyn Zeman) abusive husband D.L. Brock. Kristin Davis, whose character Brooke Armstrong on *Melrose Place* was responsible for bringing Jack back into Amanda's life, had a small role as nurse Betsy Chilton on *General Hospital* during the early '90s. Amanda's current husband on the show, Dr. Peter Burns, is played by yet another *GH* alumnus, Jack Wagner.

Melrose Place executive producer Aaron Spelling has long mined daytime for actors to star in his prime-time soaps. His first daytime find was Emma Samms, who played Robert Scorpio's former con artist wife Holly. In 1985, Spelling stole her away from *General Hospital* to take over the role of *Dynasty*'s Fallon Carrington Colby, vacated by Pamela Sue Martin. Samms later wound up on another Spelling soap, *Models Inc.*, where she played the presumed dead Grayson Louder, who turned the modeling agency into a call girl ring. (Shortly before joining *Models Inc.*, Samms had returned to *General Hospital* to resurrect the presumed-dead Holly.)

Among the latest *GH* alumni to wind up in Spelling prime-time soaps have been Paul Satterfield Jr. (ex-*Paul Hornsby*) and Alexia Robinson (ex-*Meg Lawson*), who have been cast as con man Tom Massick and special agent Cassie Wheeler respectively in *Savannah*, as well as Finola Hughes (ex-*Anna Devane*), who stars in *Pacific Palisades*.

During the mid-'80s, Tia Carrere, who played Jade Soong, niece of Asian mob leader Mr. Wu, tried to get out of her contract with *General Hospital* to join the cast of the action-adventure series *The A-Team*. Although she didn't succeed in leaving *General Hospital*, her career has not suffered too much. She has made a number of hit feature films, among them *Wayne's World*, *Wayne's World 2*, *Rising Sun*, and the Arnold Schwarzenegger action flick *True Lies*. The same Asian quarter crime story that introduced Tia Carrere as Jade also featured in a much smaller role Dustin Nguyen, who two years later would star on the Fox crime series *21 Jump Street*.

Multiple Emmy winner Tyne Daly (*Cagney and Lacey*)

checked into *General Hospital* briefly in the late '60s as Caroline Beale, a mother suffering from kidney failure.

Among the most interesting careers *General Hospital* has launched has been that of Richard Simmons, who played himself on the show from the late '70s to the early '80s. A weight-loss guru, Simmons taught exercise classes in the local disco. His popularity on the show made a best-seller out of his weight loss guide *Never Say Diet* and landed him his own syndicated fitness series, *The Richard Simmons Show*, which aired from 1980–84.

Distinguished Alumni II

Match up these actors and actresses currently on other soaps with their roles on *General Hospital*. (Answers on page 194.)

1. John Callahan (Edmund Grey, *All My Children*)
2. Robin Mattson (Janet Green, *All My Children*)
3. Ian Buchanan (Dr. James Warick, *The Bold and the Beautiful*)
4. Lilly Melgar (Claudia Cortez, *The Bold and the Beautiful*)
5. Kurt McKinney (Matt Reardon, *Guiding Light*)
6. Liz Keifer (Blake Lindsey Marler, *Guiding Light*)
7. Leigh McCloskey (Kurt Costner, *The Young and the Restless*)

a. Lily Rivera Corinthos
b. Damian Smith
c. Carla Greco
d. Leo Russell
e. Dawn Winthrop
f. Jake Meyers
g. Heather Webber

8. Sharon Case (Sharon
   Newman, *The Young
   and the Restless*)
9. Sam Behrens (Gregory
   Richards, *Sunset Beach*)
10. Laura Harring (Paula
    Stevens, *Sunset Beach*)

h. Ned Ashton

i. Sister Camellia
   McKay
j. Duke Lavery

The Movie Queens

*G*eneral Hospital has set a number of actresses well on their way to a career in feature films—namely Demi Moore, Janine Turner, and Tia Carrere. Over the years, the show has also been blessed with the talents of a number of actresses who had already made their mark in movies before coming to daytime.

Anna Lee (*Lila Quartermaine*) had finished up a thirty-five-year film career ten years before joining the cast of *General Hospital*. She worked in films in her native England from 1932 (when she made *Ebb Tide*) until 1940, when she made her first American film, the Marlene Dietrich/John Wayne drama *Seven Sinners*. During this period, she made a number of films with her then husband, director/screenwriter Robert Stevenson, among them *The Man Who Lived Again*, *Non-Stop New York*, and *King Solomon's Mines*—which starred Cedric Hardwicke as a character named Allan Quartermaine. In 1941, Lee appeared in the Oscar-winning Best Picture *How Green Was My Valley*. During the '40s, she worked with Boris Karloff in the thriller *Bedlam* and appeared in the supernatural comedy *The Ghost and Mrs. Muir*. In

Anna Lee (*Lila Quartermaine*), pictured here with on-screen husband John Ingle (*Edward*), began her film career more than sixty years ago. 1996/Cathy Blaivas/ABC

the 1960s, she landed small roles in a number of classic films. She was a nun in the Julie Andrews musical *The Sound of Music* and the next door neighbor in the Bette Davis/Joan Crawford thriller *Whatever Happened to Baby Jane?* Lee made her last film in 1968, another Julie Andrews movie titled *Star*. Twenty-five years later, in 1993, she finally got her star on Hollywood's Walk of Fame.

Anna Lee, though, was not the first movie actress to make her way onto *General Hospital*. One of the show's premiere cast members was Mae Clark, who played tough-as-nails Nurse Marge. Clark, whose film career spanned forty years, is best remembered for the breakfast scene in *The Public Enemy* where Jimmy Cagney pushed a grapefruit into her face. In addition to *The Public Enemy*, Clark had worked in such classics as *Frankenstein* and *Singin' in the Rain* as well as such medical dramas as *Magnificent Obsession* and *Not as a Stranger*. She also worked with Anna Lee in the war drama *Flying Tigers*. Clark lasted only a few months on *General Hospital*. She wanted a contract that the show could not afford to give her. After leaving the soap, she made a few more films, including the Julie Andrews comedy *Thoroughly Modern Millie* and the socially conscious *Watermelon Man*.

For the past thirteen years, Anne Jeffreys has been recurring as the socialite Amanda Barrington, an old friend of Lila Quartermaine. Like Anna Lee, Jeffreys's movie career stretches all the way back into the 1940s, when she made twenty-five films, among them *Tarzan's New York Adventure*, *Zombies on Broadway*, *Dillinger*, and *Billy the Kid Trapped*. She is best remembered as Tess Trueheart, whom she played in a number of Dick Tracy films during the decade. During the '50s, Jeffreys moved into television, starring in the supernatural comedy *Topper* as well the short-lived sitcom *Love That Jill*, which she did with her husband, Robert Sterling. Jeffreys played a faded movie queen on an episode of *L.A. Law*, and continues to appear in the occasional film. In 1994, she was seen in the Martin Short/Charles Grodin comedy *Clifford*.

In 1944, Janis Paige (*Aunt Iona Hutchison*) appeared in three films, among them the all-star musical *Hollywood*

Canteen and the Esther Williams vehicle *Bathing Beauty.* While she made movies of all types between the mid-'40s and late '60s, she is best known for musicals such as *Love and Learn, Two Gals and a Guy, One Sunday Afternoon,* and *Silk Stockings.* In 1963, the year that *General Hospital* debuted, Paige played a mental patient in the medical drama *The Caretakers,* which starred Joan Crawford as a nurse. In the early '60s, she had also starred in a couple of popular comedies, *Please Don't Eat the Daisies,* and the Bob Hope film *Bachelor in Paradise.*

Rosalind Cash (*Mary Mae Ward*) played Charlton Heston's wife in the 1971 futuristic adventure *The Omega Man.* During the 1970s, she made a number of action films and comedies, working opposite Bill Cosby twice: once in *Hicky and Boggs,* the other in *Uptown Saturday Night.* Her last feature, the anthology horror flick *Tales from the Hood,* was released after she had started working on *General Hospital.*

Stella Stevens (*Jake,* the bartender) made her film debut as Appasionate Von Climax in the 1959 movie adaptation of the Broadway musical *Li'l Abner.* During the 1960s, she got to work with Elvis Presley in *Girls! Girls! Girls!* Among her other notable films have been Jerry Lewis's *The Nutty Professor,* the disaster flick *The Poseidon Adventure,* and the Peter Bogdonavich drama *Nickelodeon.* Stevens has worked behind the camera as well as in front of it. She produced and directed the 1979 documentary *The American Heroine.* Ten years later, she directed her first feature-length film, *The Ranch,* which starred her son, Andrew Stevens.

Out of the Night

Match up the following *General Hospital* actors, past and present, with the prime-time series in which they starred before coming to daytime. (Answers on page 194.)

1. David Groh (*D.L. Brock*)
2. Brian Patrick Clarke (*Grant Putnam/Grant Andrews*)
3. David Doyle (*Ted Holmes*)
4. Mark Goddard (*Derek Barrington*)
5. Michael Cole (*Harlan Barrett*)
6. Arte Johnson (*Finian O'Toole*)
7. Don Galloway (*Dr. Buzz Stryker*)
8. Martin E. Brooks (*Dr. Arthur Bradshaw*)
9. John J. York (*Mac Scorpio*)
10. Joseph C. Philips (*Justus Ward*)

a. *Lost in Space*
b. *The Bionic Woman*
c. *The Cosby Show*
d. *The Mod Squad*
e. *Eight Is Enough*
f. *Laugh-In*
g. *Rhoda*
h. *Charlie's Angels*
i. *Ironside*
j. *Werewolf*

The Luke and Laura Quiz

Luke and Laura remain the most well-known couple in the history of daytime television. Even people who have never watched an hour of daytime television in their lives know who Luke and Laura are. This quiz is designed to see how well a fan of the show knows its premiere couple. (Answers on page 194.)

1. What is Luke Spencer's middle name?
(a) Antonio (b) Octavio (c) Lorenzo (d) Mario

Although Luke and Laura's (Tony Geary and Genie Francis) wedding was the most popular in daytime history, it wasn't the most legal. The type of divorce Laura got from Scotty could be declared null and void if he contested it, thereby nullifying her marriage to Luke as well.
1981/Bob D'Amico

2. Which of the following was never one of Laura Spencer's last names?
(a) Baldwin (b) Vining (c) Webber (d) Hardy

3. In what state did Luke and Bobbie grow up?
(a) Maine (b) Oregon (c) California (d) Florida

4. To what standard did Luke and Laura dance around Wyndham's department store?
(a) "Fascination"   (b) "It Had to Be You"
(c) "Someone to Watch Over Me"
(d) "All the Way"

5. What did Luke slip on Laura's finger as a symbol of their commitment the night after they made love in Beecher's Corners?
   (a) the pull tab from a can of soda
   (b) a ring he'd found in a box of Cracker Jack
   (c) a cigar band   (d) an onion ring

6. What did Luke rename the Cassadine yacht when the government gave it to him?
   (a) *Fancy Face*   (b) *The Haunted Star*
   (c) *The Sun Princess*   (d) *Lady Laura*

7. What were the weather conditions the night Laura disappeared in 1982?
   (a) snowing   (b) foggy   (c) torrential rains
   (d) a beautiful moonlit night

8. Where were Luke and Laura reunited when she "returned from the dead" in 1983?
   (a) the mayor's mansion
   (b) the emergency room at General Hospital
   (c) in the abandoned Campus Disco
   (d) Kelly's diner

9. What sort of business were Luke and Laura running in Canada when Frank Smith blew up their truck?
   (a) florist shop   (b) motel   (c) diner   (d) general store

10. Why did Laura throw Luke out of the house in 1995?
   (a) She caught him kissing Lucy Coe.
   (b) He had developed a gambling problem.
   (c) He had mortgaged the house to open his blues club.
   (d) His mob connections put their children at risk.

The Aztec Princess and the Rock Star. 1984/ABC

Isn't It Romantic?

While Luke and Laura remain the most popular couple in daytime history, they are not the only couple that the show's fans have fallen in love with. The following quiz salutes some of the best-loved couples in the show's history. (Answers on page 194.)

1. The romance between Steve and Audrey was the show's first real love story and its longest running. Although Audrey divorced Steve and married two other doctors before getting back together with him, she loved him right up until the day he died. Who gave Audrey away the first time she married Steve?

(a) Jessie Brewer   (b) Lee Baldwin
(c) her sister Lucille
(d) no one—she walked down the aisle alone

2. The biggest obstacle in Rick Webber's marriage to Lesley was his lingering feelings for his ex-lover Monica Quartermaine. One night, after a particularly stressful heart operation, Rick and Monica slept together. Rick and Lesley divorced but remarried several years later. How did Lesley learn that Monica thought Rick was the father of her baby?

(a) Monica referred to the child as Rick's son while Lesley was delivering the baby.
(b) Monica let her suspicions slip during an argument with Lesley.
(c) Lesley discovered Monica's request form for a paternity test.
(d) Amy Vining, who had been spying on Rick and Monica, told her.

3. Alan and Monica Quartermaine have weathered numerous affairs, murder attempts, breast cancer, their son's alcoholism, and most recently, Monica's lawsuit for sexual harassment. Yet, they have remained together. What, however, caused their divorce in the early '90s?

(a) Monica's fling with Ned
(b) Alan's affair with Lucy Coe
(c) Alan's bout with amnesia

(d) Alan's refusal to allow Monica's daughter Dawn
to live with them

4. Before there was Luke and Laura, there was Scotty and
Laura. Although Scotty never brought down any crime families, the two did see their share of danger. It was Scotty who
rescued Laura from a prostitution ring after she ran away to
New York City. Where were Scotty and Laura married?
   (a) in Rick and Lesley's living room
   (b) in the chapel at General Hospital
   (c) in the park   (d) in Las Vegas

5. Just as Scotty lost Laura to Luke, Luke lost Holly
Sutton to his best friend, Robert Scorpio, who married
Holly while Luke was presumed dead. By the time Luke
returned to town, she had already fallen in love with her
husband. Why did Robert and Holly marry?
   (a) They married while on a bender after Luke's
       memorial service.
   (b) Holly was pregnant with Robert's child.
   (c) They married to keep Holly from being deported.
   (d) They married to keep Robert from having to
       testify against Holly at her fraud trial.

6. Frisco and Felicia took over the show's crown as the
action-adventure couple in the mid-to late '80s. She was an
Aztec princess in search of her family's long-ago stolen
treasure. He was a rock-and-roll singer, who had come into
possession of a ring that held a key to finding that treasure.
How was Felicia dressed when she and Frisco first encountered one another?
   (a) as a hooker   (b) as a boy   (c) as a nun
   (d) as a police officer

7. Anna Devane was a former spy turned jewel fence turned police commissioner. It was while investigating the mysterious Mr. Big that she fell in love with mobster Duke Lavery. What was Duke and Anna's signature dance?

(a) the waltz   (b) the tango   (c) the samba
(d) the Texas two-step

8. Brenda Barrett's relationship with mobster Sonny Corinthos has nearly cost her her life on more than one occasion. She's been shot at, run over, and trapped in an underground cave-in—all at the hands of Sonny's various associates. What, however, caused Sonny to throw Brenda out of his apartment?

(a) She freed Jagger from where Sonny was
     keeping him prisoner.
(b) She refused to lie for Sonny at his trial.
(c) She allowed Mac to search the place without a
     warrant.
(d) She wore a wire for Sonny to confess his
     crimes on tape.

9. Lois fell in love with Ned Ashton and married him thinking that he was Eddie Maine, a pharmaceutical salesman by day, rock singer by night. It took Ned several months after the truth came out to win Lois back. Lois was more than a little ticked not only that her Eddie was really Ned Ashton, but that he had a second wife living in the Quartermaine mansion with him. Who did Ned marry while already married to Lois?

(a) Katherine Bell   (b) Jenny Eckert
(c) Julia Barrett   (d) Dawn Winthrop

10. Ex-psychiatrist Kevin Collins and cosmetics queen Lucy Coe have made such a poular couple on *General Hospital* that the producers have entrusted their characters with the task of launching the spin-off *Port Charles.* Because of her devotion to Kevin, Lucy named her pet duck after which famous psychiatrist?

(a) Sigmund Freud   (b) Anna Freud

(c) Carl Jung   (d) Dr. Joyce Brothers

First, Do No Harm

"First, do no harm . . ." reads the Hippocratic oath that all doctors swear before taking over their calling. A few of the doctors who've stalked the halls of *General Hospital* must have had their fingers crossed during that part of the ceremony.

Ryan Chamberlain (Jon Lindstrom) was a gifted pediatrician who once saved Robin Scorpio's (Kimberly McCullough) life. He was also a serial killer preying upon young, blond women who reminded him of the mother who had molested him. Among his intended targets was Felicia Jones (Kristina Wagner), who had witnessed him commit a murder. Ryan also brutalized Steve and Audrey Hardy (John Beradino and Rachel Ames) in their own home and later killed Jessica Holmes (Starr Andreef), the district attorney who had prosecuted him for murder. Ryan escaped from the sanitarium where he'd been sentenced several times, once by impersonating his twin brother Kevin Collins; another time by faking his own death. He rewarded Connie Cooper (Amy Benedict), the social worker who helped him escape, by strangling her with a scarf he had knit for her. Once again impersonating Kevin, he kidnapped Felicia's new-

Pierce Dorman (Tuc Watkins) sued Monica Quartermaine (Leslie Charleson) for sexual harrassment and sold drugs to her daughter Emily. 1996/Cathy Blaivas/ABC

born baby Georgie. Ryan died when the funhouse to which he had lured Felicia, Mac (John J. York), Kevin, and Lucy (Lynn Herring) went up in flames.

When psychiatrist Kevin Collins showed up in town, a few people had a hard time getting past the unnerving resemblance to his homicidal twin brother Ryan Chamberlain. After a few months, Kevin and Ryan seemed to be the classic soap opera twins: one good, the other evil. A year after Ryan died, Kevin entered a study on twins and began to experience manic episodes. About this same time, a cruel but clever prankster was stalking Felicia Jones. Audience members were left wondering if maybe Kevin was in fact Ryan and that it was Kevin who'd died in the funhouse fire. As it turned out, the twin studies had brought up Kevin's own guilt over what had happened to Ryan as a child. Just as Felicia's resemblance to their mother had inspired Ryan's original reign of terror against her, that resemblance made her a target for Kevin's troubled mind as well. He eventually took Felicia hostage in his family home.

Shortly after Dr. Kevin O'Connor (Kevin Bernhard) joined the staff at General Hospital, people from his hometown of Laurelton started turning up dead in Port Charles. Among his victims was his wife Terry's (Robyn Bernard) grandmother, Jennifer Talbot (Martha Scott), who was killed with a hypodermic needle. Jennifer's will left half her estate to Kevin and made him the prime suspect in her murder. Although Kevin went on trial for Jennifer's murder, perjured testimony from his secret lover Lucy Coe (Lynn Herring) set him free. Intending to get his hands on the rest of Jennifer Talbot's estate, Kevin began gaslighting Terry, making her believe that she had committed the murders around town. On their belated honeymoon to Catalina, Kevin tried to manipulate Terry into writing a confession and then committing suicide. Terry instead sent him falling to his own death off the side of a cliff.

Alan Quartermaine (Stuart Damon) was his wife Monica's (Leslie Charleson) biggest supporter during her life-and-death battle with breast cancer. Some fifteen years previously, though, during their first marriage, Alan was actually plotting to do in Monica and her lover, Rick Webber (Chris Robinson). Believing that Rick was, in fact, Alan Junior's biological father, Alan scheduled Rick and Monica's death during the party after the baby's christening. He rigged the ceiling in the nursery to collapse, then asked Monica and Rick to meet him there. When Alan realized that lawyer Lee Baldwin (Peter Hansen) was suspicious of him, Alan raced to the nursery and pushed Rick and Monica out of the way just as the ceiling was collapsing. He later concluded that the only way to kill Rick and Monica without going to jail would be if he caught them in bed together and shot them in the heat of passion. So Alan followed the lovers around the docks one afternoon waiting for them to go to bed. An explosion knocked Alan unconscious as he was climbing the stairs to Rick's apartment. Monica eventually tricked Alan into confessing his crime on tape but learned that the tape would not be admissable in court.

Cardiologist Phil Brewer (originated by Roy Thinnes) repeatedly cheated on his wife Jessie Brewer (Emily McLaughlin). When she filed for divorce, he got drunk and forced himself on her. Years later, after realizing that he was no longer impotent, Phil (then played by Martin West) raped his one-time lover Diana Taylor (Valerie Starrett). Both rapes resulted in pregnancy.

Pierce Dorman (currently played by Tuc Watkins) was first introduced not as an evil doctor but as an uncaring one. He refused to operate on Stone Cates (Michael Sutton) because Stone was suffering from AIDS. As time wore on, Pierce lured colleague Monica Quartermaine into an affair by acting as her secret admirer. When Monica broke off the affair, Pierce did not take it too well and began plotting revenge. He eventually sued Monica, his superior, for sexual harassment and seduced an insecure nurse into testifying against Monica. As if that wasn't bad enough, Pierce was also revealed to be the criminal mastermind bringing heroin into Port Charles.

General Hospital's Best Murder Mysteries

Who Killed Diana Taylor? (1981)

One of the more interesting elements to the Diana Taylor (Brooke Bundy) murder was the fact that the audience didn't realize there was any mystery to it until it was almost solved. For months, the audience had watched mental patient Heather Webber (Robin Mattson) plot her escape from the hospital where she'd been committed. She intended to kill Diana, who was raising Heather's biological son, Stephen Lars, and frame her other nemesis, Anne Logan (Susan Pratt), who had fallen in love with Heather's husband Jeff (Richard Dean Anderson). In one of daytime's most chilling scenes, Heather wrote Anne's name on Diana's kitchen floor, using Diana's own blood and lifeless hand. Naturally, the audience assumed that Heather had killed Diana as well. Heather, who suffered an amnesiac blackout, had assumed as much. The killer, though, turned out to be Heather's long-suffering mother, Alice Grant (Lieux Dressler). Alice had come upon Heather

When Susan Moore was murdered, her husband Scotty Baldwin (Kin Shriner) and his girlfriend Heather Webber (Robin Mattson) were prime suspects. 1982/Erik Hein

and Diana in a standoff, holding guns on each other. While Alice wrestled the gun away from Diana, it had accidentally fired.

Who Killed Susan Moore? (1983)

Heather was once again a murder suspect when her cousin Susan Moore (Gail Rae Carson) was found shot to death in her own cottage. Not only had Heather been sleeping with Susan's husband, Scotty Baldwin (Kin Shriner), Susan was threatening to press charges against the two of them for illegally dipping into her son Jason's trust fund. Also on the suspect list was the entire Quartermaine clan. Susan, still angry at Alan (Stuart Damon) for dumping her to go back to his wife Monica (Leslie Charleson), came upon some documents that could bring the family down. Lila Quartermaine's (Anna Lee) first husband Crane Tolliver (Wiley Harker) had shown Susan that he and Lila had never legally divorced, which nullifed her marriage to Edward (David Lewis) and made their children, Alan included, illegitimate and placed their inheritance in jeopardy. (According to a stipulation in Edward's father's will, Quartermaine money was only to be passed along to legitimate heirs.) Although Scotty was arrested for the crime, it was Susan's partner in crime, Crane Tolliver, who did her in after he learned that she planned to forego the blackmail money in order to expose the Quartermaines' secret purely for the thrill of revenge.

Who Killed John Prentice? (1967)

General Hospital's first murder mystery placed heroine Jessie Brewer (Emily McLaughlin) on trial for the murder of her second husband, Dr. John Prentice (Barry Atwater). When John died, everyone assumed that it was natural causes; John had been dying from a heart ailment when Jessie married him. After the autopsy revealed that John had died not from his heart condition but from a combination of barbituates and alkaloids, suspicion fell on Jessie. It didn't help her case that John had recently rewritten his will, leaving his entire estate to her. John's daughter Polly all but sent

Jessie to prison with her lies that Jessie had been carrying on with Dr. Tom Baldwin (Paul Savior) while she was married to John. Tom Baldwin ended up being charged with murder as well. In an interesting twist, it was Jessie's ex-husband Phil (Roy Thinnes) who worked to free her. He discovered that John had been experimenting with the heart medication that killed him, and that Polly—not Jessie—had given him the fatal dose.

Who Killed Phil Brewer? (1974)

Years after being convicted of killing husband John Prentice, Jessie was arrested for the murder of ex-husband Phil Brewer (played then by Martin West). By the mid-1970s, a number of people wanted Phil dead. Phil had raped and impregnated Diana Taylor (played then by Valerie Starrett). He also knew that her husband, Peter Taylor (Craig Huebing), had impregnated nurse Augusta McLeod (Judith McConnell) and was threatening to tell Diana the truth. Dr. Jim Hobart (James B. Sikking) blamed Phil for ruining his medical career. It was Jessie, though, whom Steve Hardy (John Beradino) had discovered holding Phil's lifeless body, apologizing to it. Jessie was freed only after Diana confessed to the murder and produced the murder weapon, a geode—but she wasn't the killer. She only confessed to protect her husband Peter, whom she believed had done Phil in. Jim Hobart, who worried that he might have killed Phil during one of his alcoholic blackouts, finally remembered seeing Augusta McLeod with Phil the night he was killed. Augusta ultimately confessed that she had hit him over the head with the geode to keep him from telling Diana about her pregnancy.

Who Killed Peggy Nelson? (1971)

The murder of Peggy Nelson (Ann Morrison) was just another twist in Audrey Baldwin's (Rachel Ames) attempt to keep her son Tommy away from her husband Tom. Audrey had married Tom to get over her feelings for Steve Hardy, but soon realized that she not only still loved Steve, she hated her new husband. When she discovered that she was pregnant by Tom, she left town and came back a few months later with the sad news that her baby had died at birth. In truth, Audrey had given birth to a healthy baby boy, whom an elderly woman named Peggy Nelson was minding across town for her. Audrey intended to divorce Tom, then adopt her own baby. The plan might have worked had Peggy Nelson turned out to be more of a benevolent nanny. As soon as Peggy realized Audrey's game, she wanted money to keep quiet. When Peggy Nelson was found dead, Audrey was convicted of murder. Even the audience, who had seen Audrey hide a gun in the tank of her toilet, was left wondering if she might have actually committed murder. As it turned out, Peggy Nelson had been killed by her ex-husband.

Who Killed Bradley Ward? (1993)

The Bradley Ward mystery stood out in part because the victim had never been a character on the show. He had only been seen in flashbacks. While planting flowers in their backyard, Luke and Laura Spencer (Tony Geary and Genie Francis) discovered the body of Bradley Ward, a city councilor and black activist, who had been missing since the early '70s. Edward Quartermaine (played now by John Ingle) had been a political adversary of Bradley Ward, whose political views posed a threat to Edward's business dealings. When a gun from his collection turned out to be the murder weapon, Edward went on trial for the twenty-year-old murder. Soap opera murder trials are usually highlighted with a revealing secret or two, and Mary Mae Ward (Rosalind Cash) dropped one of the biggest to hit Port Charles: Edward Quartermaine was her son Bradley's biological father. She thought that the truth would clear Edward. The prosecutor, however, turned Mary Mae's testimony around, presenting it as further motivation for why Edward would have killed Bradley Ward: namely, to keep anyone from learning that he had a biracial child. The jury thought better of Edward than that and found him not guilty. Bradley, it turned out, had been killed by Edward's long-time business associate Jack Boland (Tim O'Connor), who in turn had been killed by a hit man working for mobster Frank Smith (Mitchell Ryan).

Who Killed Damian Smith? (1996)

Almost everyone in town had motive for wanting Mafia prince Damian Smith (Leigh McCloskey) dead. He had seduced Bobbie Jones (Jacklyn Zeman) on a bet; he had blackmailed his way into ELQ; he had sent the mob after Lucy Coe (Lynn Herring); and the bad blood between Damian and the Spencers dated back to the time when Luke and Laura (Tony Geary and Genie Francis) sent his mobster father to prison. The Smith/Spencer feud hit a new low when Smith tried to get his hooks into Luke and Laura's son Lucky (Jonathan Jackson) by paying off his gambling debts. After Damian was found bludgeoned to death in the Bradley Ward house, which he had been trying to burn to the ground, Luke Spencer expected to be arrested. The police, however, arrested Laura, whose fingerprints were found on the murder weapon, a baseball bat. Family friend and lawyer Justus Ward (Joseph C. Phillips) defended Laura but hid a damning secret. He was the one who had killed Damian when he caught him setting the Bradley Ward house on fire.

Two of the best murder stories in *General Hospital*'s history were not mysteries—at least not to the audience.

The Murder of David Hamilton (1978)

This was the story line that turned *General Hospital*'s ratings around in the late '70s. Rick Webber's (Michael Gregory) friend David Hamilton (Jerry Ayres) became obsessed with Rick's new wife Lesley (Denise Alexander). When Lesley rebuffed his advances, he turned his attention to her underage daughter Laura, who was charmed by the attentions of an older man. Right before he planned to leave town, he told Laura the truth, that he was only using her to get back at her mother. Angry, Laura pushed him and he fell against the fireplace and hit his head. Lesley, who had gone to David's apartment looking for Laura, found David dead. Believing that Laura had killed David on purpose, Lesley took the blame. She tried to make it appear that she had killed David while he was trying to rape her, but her story did not jive with the evidence. She was sentenced to prison. Laura, meanwhile, had blocked out the entire incident. After her memory came back, she eventually confessed the truth and was put on probation.

The Murder of D.L. Brock (1985)

D.L. Brock (David Groh) had been physically abusing his wife Bobbie and threatening to reveal Ginny Blake

In between plotting world domination and Anna's (Finola Hughes, pictured here) kidnapping, Cesar Faison (Anders Hove) wrote romance novels. 1990/Craig Sjodin/ABC

Webber's (Judith Chapman) criminal past. One night after Brock lost control and knocked Bobbie unconscious, Ginny showed up at his apartment with a prop gun from the TV studio where she worked. She intended to threaten Brock into keeping silent. Brock, however, owned a real gun and pulled it on Ginny. While Ginny and Brock wrestled with the gun, it went off, killing Brock. When Bobbie awoke she believed that she herself had killed her husband. Ginny further gaslighted her, drugging her coffee and slashing up photos of Brock while Bobbie was unconscious. Eventually, Ginny was found out. Bobbie's testimony about Brock's violent tendencies helped to support Ginny's claims of self-defense and set her free.

Criminal Aliases
(Answers on page 194.)

1. What last name did Tony Cassadine use while anchored in Port Charles?
   (a) Anthony   (b) Baldwin   (c) Castle   (d) Diamond

2. Which police higher-up turned out to be the notorious Mr. Big?
   (a) Alex Garcia   (b) Burt Ramsey   (c) Guy Lewis
   (d) Sean Donely

3. By what code name was international criminal Nicholas Van Buren (Joseph Mascolo) better known?
   (a) Avatar   (b) The Bear   (c) Cobra   (d) Domino

4. What Port Charles resident did con man Marco Dane claim to be when he introduced himself to Tracy Quartermaine?
   (a) Luke Spencer   (b) her son Ned Ashton
   (c) Dr. Steve Hardy   (d) Robert Scorpio

5. Under what pseudonym did former DVX agent Cesar Faison write romance novels?
   (a) Daphne Andrews   (b) P.K. Sinclair
   (c) Cassandra Fairchild   (d) Desiree

Naming Names

Around Port Charles, a name change is practically a job requirement for rock stars and mobsters. And it makes no sense to fake your own death and get a new face if you're going to be using the same old name when you return to town. (Answers on page 194.)

1. Which heroine was born with the name Elsie Mae Krumholz?
   (a) Tiffany Hill   (b) Felicia Jones
   (c) Lesley Webber   (d) Audrey Hardy

2. What is Frisco Jones's real first name?
   (a) Andrew   (b) Benjamin   (c) Christopher
   (d) Daniel

3. What given first name did Stone Cates and Sonny Corinthos share?
   (a) Steven   (b) Oliver   (c) Michael   (d) Nicholas

4. By what names did Luke and Laura go while on the run from Frank Smith's mob?
   (a) Linc and Linda Lasher
   (b) Fred and Ethel Barrymore
   (c) Alan and Monica Quartermaine
   (d) Lloyd and Lucy Johnson

5. Ned Quartermaine called himself Eddie Maine while romancing Lois Cerullo. What name did he use when he slept with Monica at the health spa?
   (a) Ward   (b) Brad   (c) Philippe   (d) Dusty

Caroline Benson (Sarah Brown) showed up in Port Charles using the name Carly Roberts. Also pictured: Rachel Ames (*Audrey Hardy*) and Jacklyn Zeman (*Bobbie Jones*). 1996/Cathy Blaivas/ABC

6. What was Blackie Parrish's real first name?
(a) Albert (b) Byron (c) Charles (d) Darren

7. What was Jagger Cates's real first name?
(a) James (b) John (c) Jason (d) Joseph

8. Which leading man returned from the dead with a new face and a new name, Jonathan Paget?
(a) Tom Hardy (b) Rick Webber
(c) Duke Lavery (d) Mac Scorpio

9. What name did Bobbie use while posing as a high-priced hooker in Florida?
(a) Angel (b) Lace (c) Desiree (d) Raven

10. Where did Carly Roberts, born Caroline Benson, come up with her new name?

    (a) It belonged to her aunt.

    (b) It was the name of a friend who had died.

    (c) It was the name of the woman who sat next to her on the bus to Port Charles.

    (d) It was the name of her favorite character on a soap opera.

Gravebusters

*D*eath is a relative concept on daytime. Even when you think you see a character die and be buried, you can never really be sure that they are really gone. And when you see their ghost walking around the mansion, you can never be sure that they aren't really hiding away on some beach in the Bahamas. The residents of Port Charles probably should have realized by now not to trust reports about foreign plane crashes. And if the best anyone can produce in the way of proof is an unidentifiable corpse, it usually isn't even worth the trip to the florist's to pick out a funeral wreath.

In 1982, when Genie Francis decided to leave *General Hospital*, newlywed Laura Spencer disappeared off the end of a pier one foggy night. After months of searching for his wife, Luke Spencer (Tony Geary) and the audience had to face the horrible truth: Laura had been killed by the mysterious David Gray (Paul Rossilli) in an unfortunate case of mistaken identity. In addition to Luke, the character who missed Laura the most was her mother, Dr. Lesley Webber (Denise Alexander). Almost two years later, Laura turned up alive. She had not been killed as everyone had been led to believe; she had been held captive by and forced to marry into the evil Cassadine family.

Two years later, Laura's mother Lesley was presumed death. Like Francis, Alexander had decided to leave the show, prompting the writers to kill Lesley in an offscreen car accident. Because viewers never actually saw the accident, many held on to the hope that Lesley might still be alive somewhere. Rumors about Lesley's resurrection began circulating as soon as Genie Francis and Tony Geary agreed to reprise their roles as Luke and Laura. Eventually, Lesley did turn up alive, thirteen years after her presumed death. Like Laura, Lesley had been held prisoner by the Cassadine family.

No sooner was Lesley discovered to be alive than both she and Laura were presumably killed a second time, when the house where Lesley was being held captive blew up. This time, the writers only made the viewers grieve a few days before revealing that both Lesley and Laura were very much alive again.

Phil Brewer (played at the time by Martin West) was the first *General Hospital* character to be killed off only to return to town a few years later. After Phil's pregnant mistress Polly Prentice (Jennifer Billingsley) was killed in a car accident, Phil fled town, unaware that the district attorney had decided not to press murder charges against him. Phil himself was later presumed killed in a plane crash. It wasn't until his widow Jessie (Emily McLaughlin) had fallen in love and married Dr. Peter Taylor (Craig Huebing) that the audience learned Phil was alive. Another car accident reunited him with Jessie. Although his head was heavily bandaged when he was taken into the hospital, his nurse, Jessie, recognized his eyes. The two reconciled briefly but eventually split. Phil was killed again and permanently in late 1974.

When David Lewis asked for his workload to be cut

Port Charles turned out in force for the not-so-dead Laura Spencer's funeral. Pictured here: Shell Kepler (*Amy Vining*), Tony Geary (*Luke Spencer*), Jonathan Jackson (*Lucky Spencer*), Senait Ashenafi (*Keesha Ward*), Joseph C. Phillips (*Justus Ward*), Wally Kurth (*Ned Ashton*), and John Ingle (*Edward Quartermaine.*)
1996/Cathy Blaivas/ABC

back for health reasons, the writers decided to kill off Edward in a plane crash. Lewis continued to work for the show, reciting his dialogue off camera while Lila spoke with his ghost. After David Lewis's health had improved to the point where he could work again, he was persuaded to come back to the show in body and voice. Edward, it was revealed, had faked his own death to protect himself and his family from an international criminal orgainization. Lewis stayed with the show another few years. When he asked to leave again, the writers chose to recast the role rather than kill Edward off again.

Emma Samms (*Holly Scorpio*) left *General Hospital* in

the summer of 1985 to work on *Dynasty*, and her leading man, Tristan Rogers (*Robert Scorpio*) left a few months later. In the story line, Holly and Robert had moved to Australia. When Rogers chose to return to the show full-time in the late '80s, the decision was made that Holly needed to be killed off in order to pair Robert up with other women. The audience, which had loved Robert and Holly together, was not going to accept Robert with another woman as long as Holly was alive. So Holly was killed in an offscreen plane crash. Ironically, the character was resurrected just a few weeks before Robert was scheduled to be killed off in a boat explosion.

Musical Talents
Among the Cast

*T*he most successful singer to emerge from *General Hospital* has been Rick Springfield, who played Dr. Noah Drake. While Springfield never sang on the show, his status as an actor on daytime's top-rated soap gave him an edge in getting to perform his songs on daytime talk shows and music programs such as *Solid Gold*. Springfield, it should be noted, did have a music career going long before joining *General Hospital*. In 1972, he released the single "Speak to the Sky," which reached number 14 on *Billboard*'s Hot 100. During his first summer on the show, though, he landed the number one single, "Jessie's Girl," which went gold. He followed that up with fifteen Top 40 singles during the '80s, including three from his feature film *Hard to Hold*. In 1982, he won a Grammy award for Best Male Rock Performer.

Jack Wagner was able to parlay his role as rock singer Frisco Jones on the show into a real-life career in music. His first single, "All I Need," made it all the way to number two on the charts, kept out of the top spot by

Madonna's mega-smash "Like a Virgin." "All I Need" was featured on his first album, which also included the songs "Sneak Attack" and "Make Me Believe It," which he had performed on the show. "All I Need" was used as a love theme for Frisco and speech therapist Tanya Roskov (Hillary Edson). In 1985, Wagner released the song "Lady of My Heart," Frisco's song for Felicia, as the flip side to "Premonition." Two years later, he released the ironically titled album *Don't Give Up Your Day Job.*

The same rock band story line that introduced Jack Wagner as Frisco was used to mark John Stamos's departure as Blackie Parrish. Stamos's first series after leaving *General Hospital* was the sitcom *Dreams,* in which he played a welder/rock musician. Although the series lasted only a month, a soundtrack was released on which Stamos performed. In 1988, Stamos also played drums with the Beach Boys on their last number one single "Kokomo."

The rock band story line introduced not only Jack Wagner as Frisco Jones but Jimmy McNichol as Josh Clayton, a bellhop from whom Blackie stole the song "Make Me Believe It." Before coming to *General Hospital,* McNichol had released a self-titled album with his sister, *Family* star Kristy McNichol, that included a remake of the Chiffons' number one hit "He's So Fine."

Shell Kepler was also involved briefly in Blackie's rock story line until Amy was fired as the lead singer for his band. The following year, Kepler formed her own band, Shell and the Crush, and released a self-titled debut album. One single was released from it, "Popular Girl."

Shaun Cassidy's character Dusty Walker was introduced

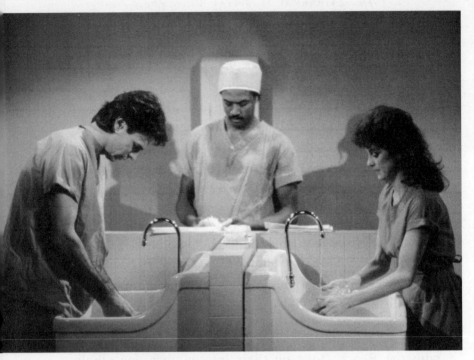

Rick Springfield, pictured here with Jacklyn Zeman (*Bobbie Spencer*), racked up hit records while playing Dr. Noah Drake but never sang on the show. 1982/Erik Hein

as a former cell mate of Blackie Parrish. While Cassidy was still starring on the teen detective series *The Hardy Boys*, he had released three Top 10 singles: the number one hit "Da Doo Ron Ron," "That's Rock 'n' Roll," and "Hey Deanie" (all three of which went gold). Dusty was paired romantically and musically with Terry Brock (played by Robyn Bernard, who has recorded gospel albums with her family).

In 1983, Nia Peeples played the short-term role of Carla Escobar, an orthopedic patient of Dr. Grant Andrews (Brian Patrick Clarke). After leaving the show, she landed a role on *Fame*, which gave her a chance to show off her singing talent. In 1988 she released the Top 40 dance hit "Trouble."

In 1993, *General Hospital* added a new dimension to business executive Ned Ashton by creating a secret life for him as rock and roller Eddie Maine. Wally Kurth was able to bring on his own band as "Eddie's" ironically titled band, the Idle Rich. He and the band have released two albums: *Kurth and Taylor* and *Half and Half*, half electric guitar songs, the other half acoustic. Kurth has performed several songs from both albums on the show, including: "Road Less Traveled," "All the Man You'll Ever Need," and "Seventh Son."

Although Edie Lehman (*Katherine Delafield*) has never released an album of her own, she has worked on several, singing back-up on two number one singles: Madonna's "Papa Don't Preach." and Belinda Carlisle's "Heaven Is a Place on Earth." She has also sung on albums by *General Hospital* cast members Jack Wagner and Rick Springfield.

Although neither the role of serial killer/pediatrician Ryan Chamberlain or psychiatrist Kevin Collins has given Jon Lindstrom much chance to show off his musical talents, Lindstrom has played drums for Los Angeles–based bands by the name of Johnny Socko and Head Seventeen. His latest group, The High Lonesome, recently released its first CD, *Feel Free to Do So*.

Paul Satterfield's (*Paul Hornsby*) biological aunt is singer Rita Coolidge ("Higher and Higher," "We're All Alone") and his stepfather is Booker T. Jones of Booker T and the MGs, who recorded the title track to the Western *Hang 'Em High*. Some of the musical talent around Satterfield rubbed off, and he released the album *Suburban Blues*.

Brad Maule, who has sung back-up for Don Ho, Bobbie

Gentry, and Jim Nabors, has gotten the chance to do a little singing as neurosurgeon Tony Jones. He has released a pair of country albums, *Living It Up* and *Chameleon*, which have garnered some airplay on country music stations.

R&B artist Keith Washington was basically playing himself on *General Hospital* as singer Keith Jasper. Exposure on the show helped his *Make It Better* go gold. The kick-off single from the album, "Kissing You," was often played as a love theme on the show. In 1993, Washington released a follow-up album and recorded a duet with Taylor Dane.

Ricky Martin, who had belonged to the Latin teen group Menudo from age twelve to seventeen, joined the cast in 1994 as Miguel Morez. Although introduced as a hospital orderly, Miguel was eventually revealed to be a singer, who stopped performing after the mob in his native Puerto Rico put out a contract on his head. Once Sonny Corinthos (Maurice Benard) called off the contract, Miguel became a popular recording artist, which Martin already was in real life. Among his releases have been a triple platinum self-titled CD as well as *Me Amaras* and *A Medio Vivir*.

Richard Dean Anderson, who played Dr. Jeff Webber, came very close to landing a record deal in the late '70s when he used to perform with the Los Angeles group Carl Dante. Carl Dante also included Emily McLaughlin's (*Jessie Brewer*) son Bob Lansing Jr. Anderson, who had sung with the group on a number of occasions, was invited along when the group headed off to Europe to record their album. Unfortunately for Anderson, the show could not afford him the time off.

In 1983 MCA released the album *Love in the Afternoon* featuring actors from all five ABC soap operas. *General*

Hospital was represented by Loanne Bishop (*Rose Kelly*) and Stuart Damon (*Alan Quartermaine*). Bishop sang "Don't Go to Strangers" while Damon covered the Kris Kristofferson classic "Help Me Make It Through the Night."

Musical Guest Stars

$\mathcal{D}$espite the wealth of talent among the cast members, *General Hospital* has occasionally imported well-known acts from the world of popular music for special occasions.

Legendary blues guitarist B.B. King performed at the opening night for Luke Spencer's (Tony Geary) new nightclub, Luke's.

Scripted as an old friend of Mac Scorpio (John J. York), pop singer Melissa Manchester ("Don't Cry Out Loud," "You Should Hear How She Talks About You") performed at his nightclub, The Outback. In real life, Manchester's manager was a cousin of one of the show's producers.

Latin balladeer Julio Iglesias ran into his old friend Ricky Martin (*Miguel Morez*) in a New York recording studio and then performed a cover of the Patsy Cline country classic "Crazy."

R&B singer Lou Rawls ("Lady Love") sang with the choir at Mary Mae Ward's (Rosalind Cash) funeral in 1996.

Folk rock singer/songwriter Janis Ian ("At Seventeen") showed up for the 1996 Nurses' Ball AIDS fundraiser and performed "When Angels Cry," which had been played during Stone's funeral.

Musical group All 4 One, seen here with Tony Geary (*Luke Spencer*), has appeared on the show twice. 1996/Cathy Blaivas/ABC

While Lois Cerullo Ashton (Rena Sofer) was bemoaning one of her many romantic problems with husband Ned (Wally Kurth), country singer Martina McBride appeared in the recording studio.

After *General Hospital* helped to turn the James Ingram/Patti Austin duet "Baby Come to Me" into a number one single, Ingram returned the favor by performing on the show during a telethon episode.

Country and Broadway singer Gary Morris has worked on a number of soaps. He played a blind singer on the prime-time serial *The Colbys* and recorded the former title track for the NBC soap *Another World*. In 1993, Morris played himself, an old friend of Tiffany Hill's (Sharon Wyatt), and serenaded the terminally ill Dominique Baldwin (Shell Danielson).

Up-and-coming R&B teen group The Boys performed at Robin's birthday party.

The pop/R&B group All 4 One performed its number one smash single "I Swear" at a benefit for the Bradley Ward House. They came back to perform at Luke's a second time during the spring of 1997.

Songs Popularized by *General Hospital*

"Faces of the Heart" by Dave Koz

When *General Hospital* was updating its opening to coincide with its thirtieth anniversary, the producers decided that a new theme song was in order to replace the ambulance siren that had been opening the show for years. The instrumental piece "Faces of the Heart" from jazz musician Dave Koz's *Lucky Man* CD was chosen for the new opening. Koz, who performed the song himself during Paul and Jenny's wedding reception, released "Faces of the Heart" as a single and filmed a music video for it, featuring *General Hospital* star Emma Samms (*Holly Scorpio*).

"Rise" by Herb Alpert

Tony Geary (*Luke Spencer*) heard the instrumental disco number "Rise" by Herb Alpert and brought it to the attention of Jill Farren, the show's music director, who agreed with him that it should be used, since the disco played such an important role in the show. The song ended up being used as background music for one of the most memorable scenes in the show's history. Luke made Laura Baldwin

(Genie Francis) dance with him to the song after the disco closed, then raped her. By the time the episode aired, "Rise" was already rising up the music charts. Exposure on the show, though, helped push the song all the way to number one and sell more than a million copies.

"Baby Come to Me" by Patti Austin and James Ingram

In the spring of 1982, the Patti Austin/James Ingram duet "Baby Come to Me" had climbed only to number seventy-three on the *Billboard* charts before falling off. That summer, it was used as the theme song between Luke Spencer and his new love interest, Holly Sutton. Exposure on the show turned the song into a slow hit. By fall, it had been rereleased and was picking up radio airplay thanks to the number of *General Hospital* fans requesting to hear it. In February 1983, almost a year after it was first released, "Baby Come to Me" was a number one single.

"Think of Laura" by Christopher Cross

In the late '70s/early '80s, Christopher Cross was a rising star with two number one singles—"Sailing" and "Arthur's Theme"—and an armful of Grammy awards for his self-titled debut album. By the mid-'80s, his career had considerably cooled. "Think of Laura," from his sophomore album *Another Page,* had not so much as cracked the Top 40. Tony Geary, though, had heard the song, and realized that it was a perfect fit for Genie Francis's return to the show in the fall of 1983. Within a few weeks of Francis's return, "Think of Laura" had reached the Top 10. It was the last hit single Christopher Cross had.

Jack Wagner (*Frisco Jones*) landed in *Billboard*'s Top 10 with "All I Need." 1985/Craig Sjodin

"General Hospi-Tale" by the Afternoon Delights

In 1980, the new wave band Planet Street set some of *General Hospital*'s story lines to music to come up with the song "General Hospital." That same year, a Boston-area radio personality by the name of Lisa Lipps set her afternoon soap updates to music and came up with the song "General Hospi-Tale." The novelty song proved so popular with the station's fans that Lipps decided to put a band together and record the song for national distribution. By the time the song was released, many of the lyrics were out-of-date, dealing with Frank Smith's mob and Monica's affair with Rick Webber. A sample stanza was filled with lines like: "Amy Vining likes to blab/Richard Simmons helps fight flab/Susan's having Alan's baby/Noah wants Bobbie for his lady." In the summer of 1981, the song cracked *Billboard*'s Top 40.

Videotapes

ABC Video has collected classic scenes from *General Hospital* together on three videotapes.

Daytime's Greatest Weddings: General Hospital was hosted by Brad Maule and Jacklyn Zeman back when Tony and Bobbie Jones were happily married. In addition to Bobbie and Tony's wedding, and, of course, Luke and Laura's 1981 extravaganza, the tape also includes clips from Laura's first wedding to Scotty Baldwin, Steve and Audrey Hardy's first wedding, Frisco and Felicia's two weddings, Alan Quartermaine's wedding to Lucy Coe, and Sean Donely's to Tiffany Hill.

Luke & Laura, Volume I: Lovers on the Run follows Luke and Laura's relationship from their first meeting right up through the point when Luke and Laura break Frank Smith's mob. Included are the classic scenes where Luke rapes Laura in the Campus Disco after hours and when the two are locked together in Wyndham's department store overnight. In addition to the highlight clips, the tape also features commentary from Genie Francis and Tony Geary.

Luke & Laura: The Greatest Love of All, Volume II, picks up with Luke and Laura's return to Port Charles after breaking Frank Smith's mob, where Laura betrayed Luke by telling the press during a conference that she was still married to Scotty Baldwin and had remained faithful to him. The tapes follows their reunion involving the Ice Princess adventure and their 1981 wedding. Unlike the clips from the *Greatest Weddings* video, these include shots of Elizabeth Taylor as Helena Cassadine. The tape moves right on through Laura's 1982 disappearance, her 1983 return from the dead, their 1985 guest spot on the show where Laura tells Luke she's pregnant, and their 1993 return to the show.

Books of Interest

General Hospital: *The Complete Scrapbook* by Gary Warner (General Publishing Group, 1995)
    Coffee-table-sized book, detailing the plotline from the very first day

Robin's Diary by Judith Pinsker and Claire Labine (Chilton, 1995)
    Paperback best-seller following the romance between Robin and and her AIDS-stricken boyfriend Stone

General Hospital series (Pioneer Books, late 1980s)
    One line in the publishers' Soaps & Serials collection, novelizing soap opera story lines—written by varied authors but edited by Mary Ann Cooper

For Richer, For Poorer; For Better, for Worse; To Love and to Cherish by Leah Laiman (Pocket Books, 1994)
    Trilogy of romance novels by former *General Hospital* writer, followed up with *The Bridesmaid* and *Maid of Honor* in the summer of 1995

Make Fashion Magic by Shell Kepler (Leisure Arts, 1996)
    Fashion designer/soap actress Shell Kepler's guide for enhancing everyday clothes

loses points for each double-cross. Among the game's more interesting rules, which would never fly on the TV series: "A character cannot marry as long as there are any undispelled rumors against him or her."

In the late '80s, United States Playing Card Company manufactured a Trivial Pursuit–styled quiz game themed around several daytime soap operas, among them *General Hospital*. Like Trivial Pursuit, the game consisted of cards containing six questions per card in such categories as romance, family ties, and legal problems. The game included "over 300 revealing questions from *General Hospital*'s provocative past and present." Although not officially associated with the Trivial Pursuit game, the question cards could be used with the board. The cards could also be played themselves and came with a custom-crafted die that featured an icon for each of the six categories on all six faces. The *General Hospital* version proved so successful that a second set of cards was issued concentrating on the 1980s.

In the early '90s, there were plans to issue a series of *General Hospital* trading cards. A couple of preview cards were included in packs of the *All My Children* cards, but the whole set was never put out.

Parodies

*I*n 1982, Garry Marshall produced the big-screen *General Hospital* spoof *Young Doctors in Love* for ABC Motion Pictures. The comedy featured the same sort of slapstick scenes, puns, and self-contained skits that made the *Airport* send-up *Airplane!* a blockbuster. Among the varied characters was a cross-dressing mobster, a direct poke at *General Hospital*'s Sally Armitage (Chris Morley), the transvestite hit man who stalked Luke and Laura during their first time on the run. Richard Dean Anderson, who had left the role of Dr. Jeff Webber the year before, had a small role in the film as a drug dealer. (Whether an intentional spoof or not, Jeff Webber had developed a drug problem during Anderson's run on the show.) The movie also included cameos by eight of the show's then current cast members: John Beradino (*Dr. Steve Hardy*), Emily McLaughlin (*Jessie Brewer*), Stuart Damon (*Dr. Alan Quartermaine*), Chris Robinson (*Dr. Rick Webber*), Kin Shriner (*Scotty Baldwin*), Jacklyn Zeman (*Bobbie Spencer*), Janine Turner (*Laura Templeton*), and Demi Moore (*Jackie Templeton*). Actors from *All My Children* and *The Young and the Restless* also had cameos. Several of the skits the *General Hospital* actors did

of Matt Fielding (Doug Savant) fell in love with a gay actor who landed a role as a doctor on an afternoon hospital soap opera. Making the connection even clearer to *General Hospital*, the show's iron-willed producer was named Gloria.

One of the more unusual comedy series on cable, *Mystery Science Theater 3000* pokes fun at bad feature films (*Godzilla vs. Megalon, The Slime People,* and *The Brain That Wouldn't Die*) by having the characters who are forced to watch them talk back at the screen. Those characters include one human, Mike Nelson, and his three robot friends, all of whom are seen in silhouette along the bottom of the TV screen. When a movie runs short, the show usually fills the gap by opening up with some sort of short subject or industrial film. In March 1994, the producers tried something a little different, broadcasting old episodes of *General Hospital* over the course of three nights. The episodes shown were first broadcast in 1964 and revolved around an engagement party that Jessie Brewer (Emily McLaughlin) was throwing for Ken Martin (Jack Betts) and Carolyn Craig (Cynthia Allison), who was seeing Jessie's husband Phil on the sly. The episode's heavy drama made it the perfect straight man for Mike and his robot friends. During a hospital scene in which one nurse hands a file to another, one of the robots shouted up at the screen: "Here are your headshots for *The Young and the Restless* audition!"

Daytime Emmy Winners and Nominees

One of the strongest campaigners for the National Academy of Television Arts and Sciences (NATAS) to recognize soap operas had been *General Hospital*'s own John Beradino. Putting his money where his mouth was, he took out ads in *Variety* and *The Hollywood Reporter,* challenging any theater, film, or prime-time actor to handle the rigors of working on a daytime soap. No one met Beradino's challenge, but in 1972, NATAS did finally recognize daytime soap operas with their own categories. In 1974, the Daytime Emmy Awards were presented in their own ceremony. Through the years, *General Hospital* has been named Best Show four times; Beradino himself was nominated three times as Best Actor.

1972: Only two soap operas were nominated for Outstanding Achievement in Daytime Drama—Programming, one of which was *General Hospital*. It lost to fellow medical soap *The Doctors*.

1974: Once again, *General Hospital* lost out to *The Doctors* in the category Outstanding Drama Series. John Beradino and Peter Hansen (*Lee Baldwin*) were both nominated in the Best Actor category but canceled each other

166/

Outstanding Daytime Drama Series. Once again producer Gloria Monty accepted the award. Stuart Damon earned his third Best Actor nomination while his on-screen father David Lewis earned his third for Supporting Actor. Loanne Bishop, who played Joe Kelly's young stepmother Rose, was nominated as Best Supporting Actress. Anne Howard Bailey and company lost the writing Emmy to Claire Labine for a second year in a row.

1985: *General Hospital* was up for Best Series but lost to *The Young and the Restless*, which had, as executive producer, H. Wesley Kenney, who would eventually take over for Gloria Monty. David Lewis was nominated for a fourth Supporting Actor Emmy. Norma Connolly (*Ruby Spencer*) was nominated for Best Supporting Actress. Jack Wagner (*Frisco Jones*) was nominated for Outstanding Juvenile/Young Man, a category which had just been introduced that year. *General Hospital* won one award, for Hairstyling.

1986: *General Hospital* was nominated for Best Series. Pat Falken Smith, who had returned as head writer, was nominated once again for Best Writing. Once again, the show won only one award, this one for Makeup. None of the actors were nominated.

1987: For the first time in almost a decade, *General Hospital* was not nominated for any Emmys.

1988: *General Hospital* was nominated for Best Show, but lost to *Santa Barbara*, which had been created and executive produced by Jerome and Bridget Dobson, whose parents created *General Hospital*. Bridget Dobson herself had once been nominated for an Emmy for writing *General Hospital*. David Lewis was once again nominated as Best Supporting Actor.

1989: Outstanding Juvenile Female Kimberly

Rena Sofer (*Lois Cerullo*) won the *Soap Opera Digest* Award as Outstanding Younger Lead Actress just a few months before she picked up her 1995 Best Supporting Actress Emmy. 1996/Dana Belcher/ABC

McCullough (Robin Scorpio) won *General Hospital* its first Emmy in three years. *General Hospital* was once again up for Best Show but once again lost to *Santa Barbara*. Interestingly, two of the Supporting Actress nominees— Jane Elliot (*Anjelica Deveraux, Days of Our Lives*); Robin Mattson (*Gina Capwell, Santa Barbara*)—had previously been nominated in the same category for their work on *General Hospital*. Nancy Lee Grahn (*Julia Wainwright, Santa Barbara*) who tied with *All My Children*'s Debbi Morgan for the Best Supporting Actress Emmy, now plays Alexa Davis on *General Hospital*. Morgan now works on the *GH*-spinoff *Port Charles*.

1990: Finola Hughes (*Anna Devane*) was nominated as Best Actress. Kin Shriner (*Scotty Baldwin*) was nominated for Best Supporting Actor but lost to *Santa Barbara*'s Henry Darrow, who had a few small roles on *General Hospital* during the mid-'80s. Two actresses from the show were nominated for Best Supporting Actress: Mary Jo Catlett, who played Katherine Delafield's maid Mary Finnegan, and Lynn Herring, who played Lucy Coe. Kimberly McCullough was once again nominated as Outstanding Juvenile Female.

1991: Finola Hughes won the Emmy as Best Actress but couldn't make it to the ceremony because she was in England, straightening out a problem with immigration. Kin Shriner was once again nominated as Best Supporting Actor as was four-time Best Actor nominee Stuart Damon. Kimberly McCullough was nominated again as Outstanding Younger Female.

1992: Lynn Herring picked up *General Hospital*'s sole nomination, for Best Supporting Actress.

1993: Gerald Anthony made Emmy history for becoming the first actor to be nominated for playing the same role

Jonathan Jackson's (*Lucky Spencer*) on-screen parents, Tony Geary and Genie Francis (*Luke* and *Laura Spencer*), presented him with his 1995 Emmy as Best Younger Actor. 1996/Dana Belcher/ABC

on two different soaps. In 1982, he earned a Best Supporting Actor nomination for playing Marco Dane on *One Life to Live*; eleven years later, he won a Supporting Actor Emmy for playing Marco on *General Hospital*. He beat out Kin

Shriner, who was up for the same award. On *General Hospital*, Anthony had worked extensively with Jane Elliot (who had returned as Tracy Quartermaine), who herself picked up a nomination as Best Supporting Actress. Doug Marland, who had made invaluable contributions to *General Hospital* in the late '70s, died in early 1993. At the Emmys that year, he was posthumously given the Lifetime Achievement Award.

1994: Sharon Wyatt, who had been working as Tiffany Hill on *General Hospital* since 1981, received her first Emmy nomination, for Supporting Actress, and *General Hospital*'s only nomination this year.

1995: The 1995 Daytime Emmys belonged to *General Hospital*, which was named Best Soap for the first time since 1984. Accepting the award was executive producer Wendy Riche and producers Julie Carruthers, Shelly Curtis, and Francesca James. James had previously won Emmys for her acting as *All My Children*'s Kelly Cole and for her directing. Claire Labine, who had won numerous Emmys for her work as creator/executive producer/head writer of *Ryan's Hope*, won *General Hospital* the Emmy for writing. In the ceremony's most touching moment, Jonathan Jackson (*Lucky Spencer*) was presented the Best Younger Actor Emmy by his on-screen parents Genie Francis and Tony Geary (*Luke* and *Laura*). Rena Sofer, who beat out cast mate Jacklyn Zeman for the Best Supporting Actress award, used her acceptance speech to clear up a rumor that she was pregnant. Brad Maule had been nominated for Best Actor, his first nomination, and Leslie Charleson for Best Actress, her first nomination since 1983. Maule was nominated for his work in the story line in which his daughter was left brain-dead in a bus accident and her heart was transplanted into her dying cousin. Charleson was nominated for Monica's battle with breast cancer. Kimberly McCullough was once again nominated as Outstanding Younger Female. *General Hospital* also picked up a technical Emmy for Costume Design.

1996: Once again, *General Hospital* was named Best Daytime Drama. Maurice Benard (*Sonny Corinthos*) earned his first Best Actor nomination. Stuart Damon and Michael Sutton, who played AIDS patient Stone Cates, vied for Best Supporting Actor but lost to *Guiding Light*'s Jerry ver Dorn. The late Rosalind Cash received a posthumous nomination as Best Supporting Actress for her work as Mary Mae Ward. Jonathan Jackson received his second daytime Emmy nomination for Best Younger Actor. Kimberly McCullough won her second Best Younger Actress Emmy for the story line in which Robin lost her boyfriend Stone to AIDS and discovered that she was HIV positive herself. The directing team picked up a nomination as well. Winning the Emmy for Outstanding Directing in a Children's Special was *Positive: A Journey into AIDS*, an ABC Afterschool Special that went behind the scenes of *General Hospital*'s AIDS story line. *Positive* was also nominated for a technical award and for Outstanding Children's Special. Once again, the show picked up the Emmy for Outstanding Costume Design.

1997: *General Hospital* was named Outstanding Daytime Drama for the third year in a row. It is now tied with *The Young and The Restless* as the soap opera named Best Show most often, each one with five awards. Sarah Brown (*Carly Roberts)* was named Best Younger Actress in her first year on the show, beating out longtime cast member and two-time winner Kimberly McCullough. The soap also picked up technical awards for Costume Design and Live and Direct to Tape Sound Mixing. Although only one actor from the show won an Emmy, approximately one-third of the cast had been nominated. Genie Francis (*Laura*

Spencer) received her first Emmy nomination—as Best Actress—but could not attend the ceremony because of her pregnancy. Francis's leading man Tony Geary was nominated as Best Actor for the first time in fourteen years. Vanessa Marcil (*Brenda Barrett*) and Jacklyn Zeman were both nominated for Best Supporting Actress; Steve Burton (*Jason Quatermaine-Morgan*) and Jonathan Jackson were nominated for Best Younger Actor; and three actors from the show were nominated in the supporting actor category: Maurice Benard, Stuart Damon, and Brad Maule, all three of whom had previously been nominated as Best Actor. They lost to *General Hospital* alumnus Ian Buchanan, who currently plays psychiatrist James Warwick on *The Bold and the Beautiful*. The show's writing and directing teams were also recognized with Emmy nominations. Hockey star Wayne Gretzky and his wife, actress Janet Jones, who are fans of the show, introduced the clips from *General Hospital*.

The *Soap Opera Digest* Awards

*N*ext to the Daytime Emmys, the *Soap Opera Digest* Awards have become the most prestigious honors for soap actors. The *Soap Opera Digest* Awards debuted in 1977 as the Soapys, and the winners were chosen purely by the readers of *Soap Opera Digest* magazine. In recent years, the awards have evolved into a combination of editors' nominations and readers' votes. From 1980 to 1983, *General Hospital* swept the awards, winning not only Best Show but the lion's share of acting honors. While *Days of Our Lives* dominated the awards from the mid-'80s to the mid-'90s, *General Hospital* was named Favorite Show in 1997 and took home one third of the evening's awards.

1979 *Winner*
Favorite Villainess: Jacklyn Zeman (*Bobbie Spencer*)

1980 *Winners*
Favorite Soap Opera: *General Hospital*
Favorite Actor: Tony Geary (*Luke Spencer*)

Favorite Mature Actor: David Lewis (*Edward
  Quartermaine*)
Favorite Juvenile Male: Philip Tanzini (*Jeremy Logan*)
An Outstanding Achievement in Daytime Award was
  presented to Emily McLaughlin, who had been
  playing Jessie Brewer since the show's premiere in
  1963.

1981 *Winners*

Favorite Soap Opera: *General Hospital*
Favorite Actor: Tony Geary (*Luke Spencer*)
Favorite Actress: Genie Francis (*Laura Webber*)
Favorite Mature Actor: David Lewis (*Edward
  Quartermaine*)
Favorite Juvenile Male: Philip Tanzini (*Jeremy Logan*)
Favorite Male Newcomer: Tristan Rogers (*Robert
  Scorpio*)
Favorite Female Newcomer: Renée Anderson (*Alex
  Quartermaine*)
Favorite Villain: Andre Landzaat (*Tony Cassadine*)
Favorite Villainess: Robin Mattson (*Heather Webber*)

1982 *Winners*

Favorite Soap Opera: *General Hospital*
Favorite Actor: Tony Geary (*Luke Spencer*)
Favorite Mature Actress: Anna Lee (*Lila
  Quartermaine*)
Favorite Mature Actor: David Lewis (*Edward
  Quartermaine*)
Favorite Villainess: Robin Mattson (*Heather Webber*)

The Casey the Alien (Bradley Lockerman) adventure won a 1991 *Soap Opera Digest* Award as Outstanding Story Line. 1990/Jerry Fitzgerald/ABC

Favorite Villain: Kin Shriner (*Scotty Baldwin*)
Favorite Male Newcomer: John Stamos (*Blackie Parrish*)

1983 Winners

Favorite Soap Opera: *General Hospital*
Favorite Actor: Tristan Rogers (*Robert Scorpio*)
Favorite Mature Actress: Anna Lee (*Lila Quartermaine*)
Favorite Mature Actor: David Lewis (*Edward Quartermaine*)
Favorite Villainess: Robin Mattson (*Heather Webber*)
Favorite Actor in a Supporting Role: John Stamos (*Blackie Parrish*)
Favorite Actress in a Supporting Role: Sharon Wyatt (*Tiffany Hill*)
Exciting New Actor: Steve Bond (*Jimmy Lee Holt*)
Exciting New Actress: Sherilyn Wolter (*Celia Quartermaine*)

1984 Winners and Runners-Up

Soap Opera Digest changed the name of its award from the Soapy to the Soap Opera Awards. While *General Hospital*'s winning streak ended, the magazine's editors presented a special recognition award to the show's executive producer, Gloria Monty. Rather than list only the winner in each category, *Soap Opera Digest* included the names of the the 1st and 2nd runners-up as well.

Outstanding Youth Actor: David Mendenhall (*Mikey Webber*)

Outstanding Actor (2nd Runner-Up): Brian Patrick
Clarke (*Grant Andrews*)

Outstanding Villain (2nd Runner-Up): Brian Patrick
Clarke (*Grant Putnam*)

Exciting New Actor (1st Runner-Up): Jack Wagner
(*Frisco Jones*)

Outstanding Actor in a Mature Role: David Lewis
(*Edward Quartermaine*)

Outstanding Actor in a Supporting Role (2nd Runner-
Up): Sam Behrens (*Jake Meyer*)

Outstanding Actress in a Supporting Role (2nd
Runner-Up): Sharon Wyatt (*Tiffany Hill*)

1985 *Winners and Runners-Up*

In 1985, *Soap Opera Digest* expanded its list of runners-up
to include the top five vote-getters in each category.

Favorite Soap (2nd place): *General Hospital*

Outstanding Actor (2nd place): Tristan Rogers (*Robert
Scorpio*)

Outstanding Actress (3rd place): Emma Samms (*Holly
Scorpio*)

Outstanding Actor in a Supporting Role (3rd place):
Brad Maule (*Tony Jones*)

Outstanding Actor in a Supporting Role (4th place):
Sam Behrens (*Jake Meyer*)

Outstanding Actress in a Supporting Role (4th place):
Hillary Edson (*Tanya Roskov*)

Outstanding Villainess (2nd place): Judith Chapman
(*Ginny Blake*)

Outstanding Actor in a Mature Role (2nd place): David
Lewis (*Edward Quartermaine*)

Outstanding Actress in a Mature Role (4th place):
Anna Lee (*Lila Quartermaine*)
Outstanding Youth Actor (2nd place): David
Mendenhall (*Mikey Webber*)
Exciting New Actress (2nd place): Kristina Malandro

1986 Winners and Nominees

In an effort to ensure a better distribution of awards to all
the shows on daytime, the editors created a list of nominees
from which the readers could then vote.

Outstanding Juvenile Actor/Actress: Kimberly
McCullough (*Robin Scorpio*)
Outstanding Daytime Serial (nominee): *General
Hospital*
Outstanding Lead Actor (nominees): John Reilly (*Sean
Donely*) and Tristan Rogers (*Robert Scorpio*)
Outstanding Actress (nominees): Judith Chapman
(*Ginny Blake Webber*), Leslie Charleson (*Dr.
Monica Quartermaine*), and Finola Hughes (*Anna
Devane*)
Outstanding Actor in a Supporting Role (nominee):
David Lewis (*Edward Quartermaine*)
Outstanding Comic Relief (nominee): David Lewis
(*Edward Quartermaine*)
Outstanding Juvenile Actor/Actress (nominee): David
Mendenhall (*Mikey Webber*)
Favorite Supercouple: Frisco and Felicia (Jack
Wagner and Kristina Malandro)

1988 *Winners and Nominees*

No awards had been presented in 1987. Changes in the voting process limited the number of nominees in each category to five.

Outstanding Supporting Actress: Anna Lee (*Lila Quartermaine*)

Favorite Newcomer: Ian Buchanan (*Duke Lavery*)

Outstanding Actress (nominee): Leslie Charleson (*Dr. Monica Quartermaine*)

Outstanding Comic Actor (nominee): Stuart Damon (*Alan Quartermaine*) and David Lewis (*Edward Quartermaine*)

Outstanding Comic Actress (nominee): Sharon Wyatt (*Tiffany Hill*)

Favorite Supercouple (nominees): Duke and Anna (Ian Buchanan and Finola Hughes) and Frisco and Felicia (Jack Wagner and Kristina Malandro)

1989 *Winners and Nominees*

Outstanding Male Newcomer: Scott Thompson Baker (*Colton Shore*)

Outstanding Villainess: Lynn Herring (*Lucy Coe*)

Outstanding Hero (nominee): Ian Buchanan (*Duke Lavery*)

Outstanding Heroine (nominee): Finola Hughes (*Anna Devane*)

Outstanding Villain (nominee): Kin Shriner (*Scotty Baldwin*)

Outstanding Comic Actor: *Stuart Damon* (Alan Quartermaine*)* and *David Lewis* (Edward Quartermaine)

Outstanding Comic Actress: Sharon Wyatt (*Tiffany Hill*)

Outstanding Female Newcomer: (nominee): Jennifer Anglin (*Cheryl Stansbury*)

Favorite Supercouple (nominee): Duke and Anna (Ian Buchanan and Finola Hughes)

1990 Winners and Nominees

Outstanding Heroine: Finola Hughes (*Anna Devane*)

Outstanding Male Newcomer: Kurt Robin McKinney (*Ned Ashton*)

Outstanding Hero (nominee) Scott Thompson Baker (*Colton Shore*)

Outstanding Actress (nominee): Leslie Charleson (*Dr. Monica Quartermaine*)

Outstanding Villain (nominee): Kin Shriner (*Scotty Baldwin*)

Outstanding Villainess (nominee): Lynn Herring (*Lucy Coe*)

Outstanding Comic Actor (nominee): Stuart Damon (*Dr. Alan Quartermaine*)

Outstanding Comic Actress (nominee): Sharon Wyatt (*Tiffany Hill*)

Outstanding Female Newcomer (nominee): Edie Lehman (*Katherine Delafield*)

Outstanding Supercouple: Colton and Felicia (Scott Thompson Baker and Kristina Malandro)

1991 Winners and Nominees

Outstanding Story Line: Casey the Alien

Outstanding Lead Actress: Finola Hughes (*Anna Devane*)

Outstanding Villain: Kin Shriner (*Scotty Baldwin*)

Outstanding Villainess: Lynn Herring (*Lucy Coe*)

Outstanding Male Newcomer: Michael Watson (*Decker Moss*)

Outstanding Hero (nominee): Jack Wagner (*Frisco Jones*)

Outstanding Supporting Actor (nominee): Bradley Lockerman (*Casey the Alien* and *Shep Casey*)

Outstanding Villainess (nominee): Jane Elliot (*Tracy Quartermaine*)

Outstanding Female Newcomer (nominee): Terri Hawkes (*Wendy Masters*)

Outstanding Supercouple: Frisco and Felicia (Jack Wagner and Kristina Malandro)

1992 *Winners and Nominees*

Outstanding Villainess: Lynn Herring (*Lucy Coe*)

Outstanding Supporting Actress: Jane Elliot (*Tracy Quartermaine*)

Outstanding Supporting Actor (nominee): Stuart Damon (*Dr. Alan Quartermaine*)

Outstanding Comic Performance (nominee): Kin Shriner (*Scotty Baldwin*)

Outstanding Male Newcomer (nominee) John J. York (*Mac Scorpio*)

Outstanding Younger Leading Actress (nominee): Kimberly McCullough (*Robin Scorpio*)

Best Wedding (nominee): Robert and Anna

Best Love Story (nominee): Mac and Dominique

1993 Winners and Nominees

Outstanding Child Actor: Kimberly McCullough (*Robin Scorpio*)

Best Social Issue Story line (nominee): A.J. Quartermaine's battle with alcoholism

Outstanding Lead Actor (nominee): Tony Geary (*Bill Eckert*)

Hottest Female Star (nominee): Emma Samms (*Holly Scorpio*)

Hottest Male Star (nominee): Antonio Sabato Jr. (*Jagger Cates*)

Outstanding Male Newcomer (nominee): Antonio Sabato Jr. (*Jagger Cates*)

Outstanding Female Newcomer (nominee): Crystal Carson (*Julia Barrett*)

Outstanding Supporting Actor (nominee): Stuart Damon (*Dr. Alan Quartermaine*)

Outstanding Supporting Actress (nominees) Jane Elliot (*Tracy Quartermaine*) and Leslie Charleson (*Dr. Monica Quartermaine*)

Outstanding Comic Performance (nominees) Kristina Wagner (*Felicia Jones*) and Kin Shriner (*Scotty Baldwin*)

Outstanding Younger Leading Actor: Steve Burton (*Jason Quartermaine*)

Outstanding Child Actor (nominee): Glenn Walker Harris Jr. (*Sly Eckert*)

Best Song (nominee): "Solo Para Tí" ("Only for You"), Holly and Simon's theme

1994 Winners and Nominees

Favorite Story Line (nominee): Dominique's death

Outstanding Lead Actor (nominee): Tony Geary (*Bill Eckert*)

Outstanding Lead Actress (nominee): Sharon Wyatt (*Tiffany Hill*)

Hottest Male Star (nominee): Antonio Sabato Jr. (*Jagger Cates*)

Hottest Female Star (nominee): Kristina Wagner (*Felicia Jones*)

Outstanding Villain/Villainess (nominee): Jon Lindstrom (*Dr. Ryan Chamberlain*)

Outstanding Supporting Actor (nominee): Wally Kurth (*Ned Ashton*)

Outstanding Scene Stealer (nominee): Gerald Anthony (*Marco Dane*)

Outstanding Younger Leading Actor (nominee): Steve Burton (*Jason Quartermaine*)

Outstanding Male Newcomer (nominee): Sean Kanan (*A.J. Quartermaine*)

Outstanding Female Newcomer (nominee): Vanessa Marcil (*Brenda Barrett*)

Outstanding Child Actor (nominee): Glenn Walker Harris Jr. (*Sly Eckert*)

Outstanding Musical Achievement (nominee): *General Hospital*

1995 Winners and Nominees

Soap Opera Digest shortened its list of nominees in each category to three, although every soap opera remained eligible for Outstanding Soap Opera. The Editors Award was presented to *Ryan's Hope* co-creator and then–*General Hospital* head writer Claire Labine.

Hottest Female Star: Kristina Wagner (*Felicia Jones*)

Outstanding Supporting Actor: Brad Maule (*Dr. Tony Jones*)

Outstanding Younger Lead Actress: Rena Sofer (*Lois Cerullo*)

Outstanding Child Actor: Jonathan Jackson (*Lucky Spencer*)

Hottest Soap Couple (nominee) Sonny and Brenda (Maurice Benard and Vanessa Marcil)

1996 Winners and Nominees

Outstanding Lead Actor: Maurice Benard (*Sonny Corinthos*)

Hottest Female Star: Lynn Herring (*Lucy Coe*)

Outstanding Supporting Actor: Stuart Damon (*Dr. Alan Quartermaine*)

Hottest Male Star (nominee): Wally Kurth (*Ned Ashton*)

1997 *Winners and Nominees*

The ceremony was held in the Amphitheater at Universal Studios and was hosted by talk show host/soap fan Leeza Gibbons along with an actor from each network including Ingo Rademacher (*Jax*), who was named Hottest Male Star.

Favorite Show: *General Hospital*

Outstanding Lead Actress: Genie Francis (*Laura Spencer*)

Hottest Male Star: Ingo Rademacher (*Jax*)

Hottest Female Star: Vanessa Marcil (*Brenda Barrett*)

Outstanding Male Newcomer: Tyler Baker (*Nikolas Cassadine*)

Outstanding Younger Lead Actor: Steve Burton (*Jason Quartermaine-Morgan*)

General Hospital Knowledge

This quiz covers *General Hospital*'s history from Steve Hardy's first on-screen romance right up to Lesley Webber's return from the dead. A score of fifteen or more is considered passing. (Answers on page 194.)

1. Why did Steve Hardy's fiancée Peg Mercer break off their engagement?
>   (a) She found him kissing Audrey March.
>   (b) She blamed him for her mother's death.
>   (c) She realized that the hospital would always come first with him.
>   (d) She discovered that she was dying from leukemia.

2. Which of her husbands did Jessie Brewer marry twice?
>   (a) Phil Brewer (b) John Prentice
>   (c) Peter Taylor (d) none of them

3. What did Audrey originally name her son Tom?
>   (a) Kenny (b) Timmy (c) Stevie (d) Petey

4. How did Lesley Webber meet Gordon Gray, her daughter Laura's biological father?
>   (a) He was her first patient.
>   (b) He was a business partner of her father.
>   (c) He was her college professor.
>   (d) He had grown up with her.

5. How was Steve Hardy paralyzed from the waist down?

> (a) He fell down a flight of stairs at General
>   Hospital.
> (b) Tom Baldwin ran him down in the parking lot.
> (c) His car skidded off the road on a rainy night.
> (d) His paralysis was psychosomatic, triggered by
>   his fear of remarriage to Audrey.

6. After running away from the Vinings, where did Laura stay?

> (a) in a seedy New York apartment
> (b) on a religious commune
> (c) with a traveling carnival   (d) in a convent

7. What was the name of the disease that quarantined General Hospital and created an epidemic in Port Charles?

> (a) Lassa fever   (b) Black fever
> (c) The Egyptian flu   (d) the dreaming death

8. What discovery gave Monica her first clue that Alan and not Rick Webber was the actual father of her child?

> (a) the baby's allergy to milk
> (b) an odd-shaped birthmark
> (c) a test result that hinted Rick could be sterile
> (d) the fact that only Alan could stop the baby from
>   crying

9. What was the left-handed boy?

> (a) a statue   (b) an antique car   (d) a racehorse
> (d) Frank Smith's code name for Luke Spencer

10. When Heather believed that she had shot and killed Diana Taylor, where did she hide the gun?

    (a) in the head of a doll

    (b) under the floorboards at Kelly's

    (c) in her mattress

    (d) in Anne Logan's closet

11. David Grey had presumably killed Laura Webber in quest to possess the Sword of Malkuth. According to legend, which historical figure had the sword belonged to originally?

    (a) Alexander the Great   (b) Mark Antony

    (c) St. George, the Dragon Slayer

    (d) King Richard the Lion Hearted

12. What was the evil spy network that Robert Scorpio was constantly battling?

    (a) the AIC   (b) the BGK   (c) the CDC

    (d) the DVX

13. Russian spies Grant Putnam and Natalie Dearborn schemed to steal an energy disk named after what mythological figure?

    (a) Mars   (b) Prometheus   (c) Mercury   (d) Zeus

14. What song did Blackie Parrish steal from bellhop Josh Clayton?

    (a) "All I Need"   (b) "Make Me Believe It"

    (c) "Sneak Attack"   (d) "Premonition"

15. What did Lila Quartermaine name the relish she invented with Stella, the maid?
      (a) Lila's Own (b) Millionaire's Choice
      (c) Pickle-Lila (d) Stellar Relish

16. What show did Colton Shore host?
      (a) *From the Heart* (b) *Common Sense*
      (c) *The Colton Connection*
      (d) *Good Morning, Port Charles*

17. From what planet did Casey the Alien come?
      (a) Alvor (b) Calliope (c) Lumina (d) Melador

18. What color dress did Lucy wear when she married Alan Quartermaine?
      (a) gold lamé (b) emerald green
      (c) black (d) red

19. What Quartermaine ship was Mac Scorpio arrested for blowing up?
      (a) The USS *Lila* (b) The *Monica*
      (c) The SS *Tracy* (d) The ELQ yacht

20. In what sport did Jagger Cates compete?
      (a) surfing (b) boxing (c) race car driving
      (d) weightlifting

21. What was the name of the strip joint that Sonny Corinthos used to run?
      (a) Sonny's (b) Hedonism (c) Paradise Lounge
      (d) The Dungeon

22. What information did Katherine use to blackmail her way into marriage with Ned?
>   (a) that Lila and Edward were never legally
>   married
>   (b) that Alan had killed Ray Conway
>   (c) that Tracy had run over Jenny Eckert in
>   her car
>   (d) that Edward had fathered a biracial child

23. What did Nikolas give Lulu for her second birthday?
>   (a) an antique rocking horse   (b) a Fabergé egg
>   (c) a silver rattle   (d) one million dollars

24. From what fear does Sonny Corinthos suffer?
>   (a) arachnophobia   (b) acrophobia
>   (c) claustrophobia   (d) hydrophobia

25. For how many years was Lesley Webber presumed dead by her family?
>   (a) 7   (b) 10   (c) 13   (d) 22

1981/ABC

Bonus question: What is this?

The Spin-Off

*O*n June 1, 1997, ABC launched the half hour *General Hospital* spin-off *Port Charles* with a two-hour Sunday night movie revolving around a hostage drama at the hospital. The soap opera began its official schedule as a daytime soap opera the very next afternoon.

The spin-off *Port Charles* marked Kin Shriner's fourth return to the role of Scotty Baldwin. He originally played Scott as a teenager from 1978 until 1980, when he left to work on *General Hospital*'s rival *Texas*—itself a spin-off from *Another World*. He came back in 1981 and stayed until 1983. Four years later, Shriner returned for his longest run, six years. It was during this time that Scotty met Lucy Coe, his future lover and the surrogate mother for his daughter Serena. In 1993, after being kidnapped by the mob, Scotty left town with his daughter.

In addition to Scotty, the two characters picked to headline the new soap are Lucy Coe (Lucy Herring) and her ex-psychiatrist boyfriend Kevin Collins (Jon Lindstrom).

One of the first actors to be hired for *Port Charles* from outside the *General Hospital* cast was Wayne Northrop, who had played police captain Roman Brady on *Days of*

Our Lives and has been married to Lynn Herring for six-teen years.

Only two other daytime soaps have spun off other soaps. In the 1960s, *As the World Turns* sent its most pop-ular heroine, Lisa Miller (Eileen Fulton) into primetime with a serial of her own, *Our Private World*. In the 1970s, *Another World* moved three characters from Bay City to nearby *Somerset*; in 1980 it shipped its lead villainess, Iris Carrington (Beverlee McKinsey) to Houston in *Texas*.

Only two other soap operas have begun in prime-time. In 1982, CBS premiered the political drama *Capitol* after an episode of *Dallas*. The following year, ABC launched *Loving* with a two-hour movie of the week.

During the height of the Luke and Laura phenomenon, the idea for a *General Hospital* sequel was first proposed. The immense popularity of Luke and Laura naturally gen-erated thought about giving them their own soap. The exec-utives at ABC wisely concluded that the loss of Luke and Laura could severely dig into *General Hospital*'s ratings. Because young viewers were responsible for much of the show's success, ABC also considered a spin-off titled *The Young Loves of General Hospital* that would focus around a new group of younger characters who would be introduced on *General Hospital* for the express purpose of being spun off into their own series. Ultimately, that idea was shot down as well.

When Gloria Monty returned to *General Hospital* in 1991, she brought on board the blue-collar Eckert family. Fascinated as she was at the time by the struggles between the various classes, she wanted to create a soap focused around the branch of the Eckert family that lived in Oregon. Unfortunately for her plans, the Eckerts never caught on with the viewers as a popular family.

Answers to the Quizzes

GETTING OUT OF TOWN FOR A WHILE (1) c (2) c (3) a
(4) c

FOREIGN SOIL (1) f (2) a (3) f (4) h (5) f (6) b (7) e
(8) d (9) j (10) g (11) c (12) i

DISTINGUISHED ALUMNI II (1) d (2) g (3) j (4) a (5) h
(6) i (7) b (8) e (9) f (10) c

OUT OF THE NIGHT (1) g (2) e (3) h (4) a (5) d (6) f
(7) i (8) b (9) j (10) c

THE LUKE AND LAURA QUIZ (1) c (2) d (3) d (4) a
(5) c (6) b (7) b (8) a (9) c (10) d

ISN'T IT ROMANTIC? (1) c (2) a (3) b (4) c (5) c (6) b
(7) b (8) d (9) a (10) a

CRIMINAL ALIASES (1) c (2) b (3) d (4) b (5) b

NAMING NAMES (1) a (2) a (3) c (4) d (5) a (6) a
(7) b (8) c (9) d (10) b

GENERAL HOSPITAL KNOWLEDGE (1) c (2) a (3) c (4) c
(5) a (6) b (7) a (8) b (9) a (10) a (11) a
(12) d (13) b (14) b (15) c (16) c (17) c (18) d
(19) c (20) b (21) c (22) b (23) b (24) c (25) c
(Photo Bonus) The Ice Princess

Index

Character names are in **boldface**. Page numbers in *italics* refer to picture captions.

backstage stories, 35–39
Bailey, Anne Howard, 165, 166
Baker, Scott Thompson, 72, 86
Baker, Tyler, 70
Baldwin, Audrey (Audrey March; Audrey Hardy), *5, 6,* 8, 9, *10,* 11, 31–32, 73, 75, 120, 128, *134,* 153, 164
Baldwin, Dominique, 72, 148
Baldwin, Gail, 71, 92
Baldwin, Laura, see **Spencer, Laura**
Baldwin, Lee, 2, *10,* 73, 123, 163
Baldwin, Scotty, 14, 15, 50, 55, 66, 73, 76, 102, 113, *125,* 126, 153, 154, 159, 168, 192
Baldwin, Tom, 11, 127, 128
Baranski, Michael, 58
Bare Essence, 78
Barrett, Brenda, 34, 54, 73, 82, *96,* 172
Barrett, Julia, 55, 66, 72, 94
Barrington, Amanda, 110
Barrington, Derek, 43
Batman, 90, 104
Batman Forever, 90
Bauer, Franz, 7
Beale, Caroline, 106
Beauty on the Go (Zeman and Whitley), 156
Beecroft, David, 75
Beecroft, Gregory, 24, 75
Behrens, Sam, 68, 72, 80
Belack, Doris, 160
Bell, Felecia, 71, 93
Bell, Katherine, *30,* 33, 64, 71, 97–98, *98*
Benard, Maurice, 64, 67, 71, 91, 93, *96,* 144, 171, 172
Ben Casey, 1

Benedict, Amy, 120
Ben Jerrod, 2
Benson, Caroline (Carly Roberts), 70, 81, *134*
Beradino, John, 1, 2, 3, *4, 5,* 7, 8, 9, *10,* 33–34, 35, 40, 48, 84, *85,* 86, 90, 120, 127, 159, 160, 163–64
Berle, Milton, 47
Bernard, Crystal, 76
Bernard, Robyn, 56, 71, 76, *77,* 122, 142
Bernhardt, Kevin, 58, 64, 122
Berra, Yogi, 48
Best, Kevin, 70
Betts, Jack, 68
Bialik, Mayim, 53
big breaks, 86
Billingsley, Jennifer, 137
birthdays, 70–73
Bishop, Loanne, 73, 145, 166
Blake, Ginny, *see* **Webber, Ginny Blake**
Blossom, 53
Blues Brothers, The, 50
Blumenthall, Jon, 156
Boland, Jack, 50, 129
Bold and the Beautiful, The, 43, 172
Bollman, Billy "Bags," 51
Bond, Steve, 20, 63, 67, *68,* 71, 82, 84, 90
books, 155–56
Bowen, Paige, 31
Boys, The, 148
Brady, Roman (*Days of Our Lives*), 79, 99, 193
Brewer, Jessie, 2, *4, 10,* 58, 59, 92, 123, 126–27, 137, 144, 159